A MESSAGE FROM
NFIB's PRESIDENT,
WILSON S. JOHNSON

Inflation, taxes and government regulation—wherever I go and whenever I speak with small business owners, those are the three concerns that constantly rise. Unfortunately, my experience is not isolated. These problems are also echoed by our NFIB District Managers, who visit thousands of small businesses throughout the country daily, and by our regular polls that are the base for the *NFIB Quarterly Economic Report for Small Business.*

Inflation, taxes and government regulations—your message is clear. At least to NFIB. But is your message clear to others, particularly those government officials in a position to do something about it? William E. Simon, a distinguished former Secretary of the Treasury, flatly warns that the answer is "no." Washington, states Secretary Simon, is still filled with "economic illiterates" who fail to recognize that billions of economic decisions made by millions of individual people in the marketplace can never successfully be supplanted by yet another government agency and a ream of new regulations.

A Time for Truth is Bill Simon's account of his traumatic fight to preserve free enterprise while holding three of the nation's highest offices. It is at the same time revealing and entertaining, humorous and maddening. Throughout, it is candid. No one who would increase government intervention in the private sector is spared—not Presidents, not Congresses, not bureaucrats, not Republicans, not Democrats, not the media, not universities, not labor unions, and certainly not businessmen desiring to warp the system for corporate advantage. But far more than an account of Bill Simon's days in Washington, *A Time for Truth* is an attack and a plan. It is an attack on economic illiteracy, the kind that fails to recognize that consistently huge federal deficits must cause inflation or that increased regulation must cause lower productivity. And it is a plan to those in business and in the public who do understand the economic facts of life to do something about the deteriorating situation.

As a service to the membership, this condensed copy of *A Time for Truth* is being provided you...READ IT! Think about what you and your fellow NFIB members have been telling us about inflation, taxes and government regulation...then write the President, write your congressmen, write your senators! Let them know how these cripplers are affecting your business.

> Wilson S. Johnson
> President
> National Federation of
> Independent Business

A TIME FOR TRUTH

WILLIAM E. SIMON

With an Epilogue by the Author

A BERKLEY BOOK
published by
BERKLEY PUBLISHING CORPORATION

A TIME FOR TRUTH

A Berkley Book / published by arrangement with
The Reader's Digest Association, Inc.

PRINTING HISTORY
Original Reader's Digest Press edition published 1978
Original Berkley edition / April 1979

ISBN: 0-425-04579-X

A BERKLEY BOOK® TM 757,375
Berkley Books are published by Berkley Publishing Corporation,
200 Madison Avenue, New York, New York 10016.
PRINTED IN THE UNITED STATES OF AMERICA

I dedicate this book to my wife, Carol, who stands by my side throughout all my battles— and to my children, so that they can never say, at some future time, "Why weren't we told?"

Acknowledgments

I wish to express my profound gratitude to Edith Efron, who assisted me with every aspect of this book, from conception to execution. The dedication to liberty which animates these pages is hers, as well as my own.

I am also deeply indebted to Managing Editor Kenneth Gilmore and Washington Editor William Schulz of the *Reader's Digest*, who spent countless hours on this project and whose guidance, criticism, and direction have been invaluable. It was they who wisely counseled me to limit the canvas of this book to domestic issues.

And finally, I wish to thank DeWitt Wallace and Hobart Lewis of the *Reader's Digest*. Without their inspiration, this project might not have been undertaken.

Acknowledgment is made for permission to reprint excerpts from the following works:

"The New Despotism" by Robert Nisbet, in *Commentary*.

Irving Kristol's "Business and 'The New Class,'" in *The Wall Street Journal* May 19, 1975. Reprinted with permission of *The Wall Street Journal* © 1975 Dow Jones & Company, Inc. All rights reserved.

"Default at the New York Times," by Martin Mayer. Reprinted from the *Columbia Journalism Review*, January/February, 1976.

"Last-Minute Bailout of a City on the Brink." Reprinted by permission from TIME, The Weekly Newsmagazine; Copyright © Time Inc., 1975.

Preface

This is a brilliant and passionate book by a brilliant and passionate man. It is a profound analysis of the suicidal course on which our beloved country is proceeding—so clearly and so simply written, with such eloquence, such obvious sincerity, such a broad base in recorded fact and personal experience, that it is hard to see how any reasonable man who wishes his fellow citizens well can fail to be persuaded by it.

MILTON FRIEDMAN

Foreword

If, when a mutual friend had given me an opportunity to read this manuscript, I had been clearly aware that it was the work of a recent Secretary of the Treasury, I doubt whether I would have been particularly anxious to read it. Remembering only that the folder contained the work of a younger man of whom my friend expected much, I dipped into it one morning and at once got so fascinated that I could not stop until I had finished it. I still know very little about the role the author played in recent American history beyond what I learned from his own account of it. All I know is that this account of his experience and the lesson he learned from it is of the greatest importance.

How a man with his views could ever have become U.S. Secretary of the Treasury is still something of a puzzle to me. But perhaps the explanation of the opinions so unlikely to be formed in such a position is probably that he was young enough to be really shocked by what he experienced and to learn what mature politicians no longer can learn: that the compulsion under which our system of unlimited democracy places persons at the head of government to operate forces them to do things which they know to be permissive, but must do, if they are to retain the position in which they can still hope to do some good.

If this is the lesson which a first-class young brain has learned from bitter experience, we may hope to find in him a leader of opinion such as the United States and the Western world much need. But at least what he tells us in this book ought to teach many what the obstacles are to a sensible policy being followed by government. I never imagined that government could harbor a spirit opposed for good reasons to so much that was in fact done.

I can assure the reader that Mr. Simon is not unduly an alarmist. If we learn from him and the few people who think like him, we may still avert the threatening collapse of our political and economic order. Without much hope I recommend this book particularly to my fellow economists who could learn much from it never dreamed of in their philosophy.

F. A. HAYEK

I

Mr. Chairman!

... government, even in its best state, is but a
necessary evil; in its worst state, an intolerable
one.

—THOMAS PAINE

If one plans to drive from Virginia into Washington, D.C., April
is the time to do it. The air is fragrant, the cherry trees are massed
along the Potomac, and the great white temples that house the
statues of Lincoln and of Jefferson glow serenely in the sun. One
April day I took this drive, and I knew that this spectacle was
outside my window, but I didn't see it. I was inside a limousine
scanning a mass of statistics, and there was no room in my
consciousness for such pleasures. It was 1976. I was Secretary of
the Treasury of the United States, the country was emerging
from a deep recession, and I was on my way to testify before a
Congressional subcommittee.

As I look back, now that I have left office, I sometimes have
the impression that that is how I spent most of my years in
Washington, from 1972 to 1977, racing to testify before assorted
groups of Senators and Representatives. I've been told that I set
the all-time record for such appearances.

But given my unique situation, it was inevitable. As fate
would have it, I made my political debut by landing in the very
eye of the two economic cyclones that swept over the country
during my years in office. I was not only Treasury Secretary
during the worst inflation and recession to rock the country in 40
years, but also the "energy czar" during the OPEC nations' oil
embargo, which dramatized to Americans for the first time that
this country had lost its energy independence. Since both our
economic condition and our energy sources were of universal

1

concern, my responsibility in these areas had given almost every committee and subcommittee in the Senate and the House the desire to question me at regular intervals for almost four years.

Most of these hearings were an abysmal waste of time. As best as I can make out, most of the Congress learned virtually nothing from them, since my answers were rarely wanted or believed. Essentially, I was always sending the Congressmen one fundamental and disagreeable message—namely, that the government in general and Congress in particular were responsible for both the economic and the energy crises and for the dangers associated with them.

Inevitably, I was not the most popular man in Washington, and I was often unpopular within the Administration itself. Republicans, like Democrats, had participated over the years in the forging of the political and legal fetters for our productive system, and like Democrats, they often demonstrated an inability to comprehend the mischief they had wrought and were still perpetuating. I found myself compelled, in 1974, to inform President Nixon that his fiscal policies were "insane" and that a balanced budget was imperative. A year later I was engaging in a verbal wrestling match with President Ford over his proposals to "liberate" energy production in this country by intensifying and expanding state control over the energy industries.

In retrospect, I cannot imagine why both Presidents maintained me as their Secretary of the Treasury rather than send me packing. It would be nice to believe that they held onto me because they believed in private that I was right. Something like that, I suspect, is the case, for I was not fired. And until my last day in office, I kept struggling to make the government grasp that *it* was the architect of our disasters.

As we approached the Cannon House Office Building that April morning, I felt a great fear for the country. That fear surfaced more vividly than usual in the testimony I gave that day. I set aside my prepared text and delivered a spontaneous speech to the listening Congressmen. It was the only time I had ever done this. I spelled out the very concerns which constitute the themes of this book:

Unfortunately, all the rhetoric about deficits and balanced budgets obscures the real danger that confronts us: the gradual disintegration of our free society.

This country is in desperate danger. The danger is obscured when we talk about deficits of $40 billion or of $70 billion or *about whether we should balance the budget. The real issue is the government's share of the Gross National Product—of the earnings of every productive citizen in this land. That is the issue on which we should concentrate. What does it mean for the American dream? What does it mean for our way of life? What does it mean for our free enterprise system? What is our free enterprise system? Isn't free enterprise related to human freedom, to political and social freedom? When we see this monstrous growth of government, we must realize that it is not a matter of narrow economic issues. What is at stake is equity, social stability in the United States of America. What is at stake is the fundamental freedom in one of the last, and greatest, democracies in the world.*

You asked, Mr. Chairman, about the consequences of deficits. But we all know what they are. We all know that neither man nor business nor government can spend more than is taken in for very long. If it continues, the result must be bankruptcy. In the case of the federal government, we can print money to pay for our folly for a time. But we will just continue to debase our currency, and then we'll have financial collapse. That is the road we are on today. That is the direction in which the "humanitarians" are leading us.

The problems of deficits, budget balancing, capital markets—all these are important. But it is more important, I think, to understand that these are just early warning symptoms of a disease that threatens the very life of our body politic. And if we continue to move down this same path, that disease will be irreversible, and our liberty will be lost. I speak of this so insistently because I hear no one discussing this danger. Congress does not discuss it. The press does not discuss it. Look around us—the press isn't even here! The people do not discuss it—they are unaware of it. No counterforce in America is being mobilized to fight this danger. The battle is being lost, and not a shot is being fired.

That, Mr. Chairman, is why for me the last few years in office have been like a bad dream. I am leaving Washington next January. I am going to go home to New Jersey a very frightened man.

I did not set out to make this speech. It was extemporaneous. The subject of the hearing was one of the most important in America's political life. But on this occasion most of the committee members had not shown up, the press had not shown up, and there sat Chairman Ichord solemnly reciting statistics. It suddenly struck me with force that this situation—an empty dais, an empty press section, and a Niagara of numbers—symbolized exactly what was occurring in the nation: an almost universal incomprehension of a glaring danger. It was that particular thought that had provoked my outburst. It expressed the essence of what I had come to understand during my years in Washington.

Those years had been intensely educational. What I had learned, above all, was that the country was in a precarious state, that its very cornerstone, economic and political liberty, had been seriously eroded. As I told the chairman of that subcommittee on that distant April day, *the reason for discussing economic issues is not to inspire a national passion for bookkeeping, but to inspire a national awareness of the connection between economic and political freedom. The connection is real and unbreakable. To lose one is to lose the other. In America we are 'losing both in the wake of the expanding state.* That was my constant thesis as Secretary of the Treasury, and that is the theme of this book. There is no surer sign of the danger we face than the fact that so cardinal a truth—that the state itself is a threat to individual liberty—should be classified today as "controversial."

II

Freedom vs. Dictatorship

> Liberty has never come from the government.... The history of liberty is the history of the limitation of governmental power, not the increase of it.
>
> —WOODROW WILSON

In April 1975, after a grade meeting in Moscow, I boarded Air Force Two with the U.S. delegation. Still caught up in our official roles, we continued to discuss the ramifications of East-West trade. Then, abruptly, the roar of the motor broke into our conversation, and as the plane taxied down the runway, we all fell silent. After a moment or two Air Force Two lifted off. We heard the dull thump of the locking wheels. The ground fell away beneath us. We were no longer on Soviet soil! And everyone burst into applause.

I'll never forget the moment of elation that possessed us all. It needed no translation. I knew exactly what the emotion was: a sense of oppression being lifted from all of us who had never known oppression. It felt, for a crazy moment, as if we were staging a great escape. I remember that sense of "I can breathe again. I can talk again. I'm not being spied on any more." It was a sudden vanishing of all the menacing things that characterize the Soviet Union, the shadowy intrusions that you can feel but cannot see. Throughout all the long, cooperative working hours, underlying the jovial ceremonies, lurking beneath the flash of crystal, the flow of vodka, the unspoken awareness of unseen oppression had been with each of us. We too had felt unfree. So all of us, 78 dignified representatives of the United States of America, shouted and applauded like youngsters in sheer relief

5

because we had emerged from that mammoth jail called the Soviet Union, because we were flying home, flying toward freedom. And it was then, for the first time, that I could put into words that sense of a deep, unnamable difference between the Soviet officials and myself. It was the difference between men who have never known freedom and men who were born free. Freedom is strangely ephemeral. It is something like breathing; one only becomes acutely aware of its importance when one is choking. Similarly, it is only when one confronts political tyranny that one really grasps the meaning and importance of freedom. What I actually realized in Air Force Two is that *freedom is difficult to understand because it isn't a* presence *but an* absence—*an absence of governmental constraint.*

Americans have had the unique privilege of living in a nation that was organized, constitutionally and economically, for one purpose above all: to protect that freedom. Our Founding Fathers, for whom the knowledge of the centuries of tyranny that had preceded them was vivid and acute, were guided in the creation of our political and economic system by that knowledge; virtually every decision they made was to bind the state in chains to protect the individual's freedom of thought, choice, and action.

I have also come to realize that of all the aspects of political freedom guaranteed to us by our Constitution, freedom of action—most particularly, freedom of productive action or free enterprise—is the least understood. For years, in Washington, I have been watching the tragic spectacle of citizens' groups, businessmen, politicians, bureaucrats, and media people systematically laying waste to our free enterprise system and our freedom even as they earnestly—and often sincerely—proclaimed their devotion to both. Again, this widespread incomprehension is largely due to the fact that freedom of action, including freedom of productive action, is simply a subdivision of freedom; it, too, is an *absence* rather than a *presence*—an absence of governmental constraint. By whatever name one wishes to call this category of free human action—free enterprise, the free market, capitalism—it simply means that men are free to produce. They are free to discover, to invent, to experiment, to succeed, to fail, to create means of production, to exchange goods and services, to profit, to consume—all on a voluntary basis without significant interference by the policing powers of the state. In the most fundamental sense, the right to freedom in this entire chain of productive action adds up to the right to life—for man, by his nature, is a being who must produce in order to live.

Our Founding Fathers, in whom I grow progressively more interested as I grow older, were well aware of this. One of the British philosophers who influenced their thought most profoundly was John Locke. And when I discovered his existence fairly recently (I was no scholar in college), I felt as if he were speaking directly for me. "A man . . . having, in the state of nature, no arbitrary power over the life, liberty or possession of another, but only so much as the law of nature gave him for the preservation of himself and the rest of mankind, this is all he doth or can give up to the commonwealth, and by it to the legislative power, so that the legislative can have no more than this."

In other words, government's power, said Locke, was logically limited to the protection of each individual's right to his life, his liberty, and his property, and any government that interfered with these rights instead of protecting them was illegitimate. It is this language that ultimately appeared in our Constitution as the rights to "Life, Liberty, and the Pursuit of Happiness." Our Founding Fathers, intellectual heirs of Locke, consciously and deliberately created the first limited government in the history of man.

A philosopher I cherish equally is Adam Smith, the Scottish theoretician of free enterprise—that political system in which the state leaves producers and consumers free to produce and consume as they choose. Smith, too, believed in the natural right of the individual to liberty, and his essential message to all government was "laissez-faire," or "leave people alone to act." In *The Wealth of Nations*, published by happy coincidence in 1776, Adam Smith denounced the "mercantilists" of his period who (precisely like our contemporary "liberals") argued that a government should control all aspects of domestic and foreign trade if it wished to enrich the nation. Smith, on the contrary, argued that if the goal were wealth, the productive individual should be free of all such state controls, in accordance with "a system of natural liberty." In total liberty, he said, wealth would necessarily be produced on a scale yet unforeseen.

Our Founding Fathers must have read *The Wealth of Nations* with great satisfaction, for, as Smith himself observed, the American colonies had been practicing what he preached for more than a century. In their dedication to individual liberty, the earliest leaders of this nation were determined to leave citizens free to seek their fortunes with a minimum of state interference, and a free-market system rooted in "natural law" had been the brilliant result. From its very birth America was a natural laboratory for the liberty-loving philosophies of such men as Locke and Smith, and this country proved to be the noblest experiment ever devised by man. Not coincidentally, it also proved to be the form of society that produced a degree of wealth and a standard of living for the "common man" that had never before been seen. America was by the very definition of its founders a capitalist nation.

The extraordinary wealth of our nation is well known throughout the world. The statistics which record the tangible results of that system nevertheless miss the invisible dimension. The single most awe-inspiring thing about our economic system lies in what is *absent*, what is *not* perceivable to the naked eye. It is the fact that the flood of wealth emerges from the lack of government control, from the lack of state-imposed or "national" purposes and goals. The capitalist miracle occurred in the United States, the politically freest nation in the world, precisely because this explosion of wealth is uniquely a result of *individual liberty*. That is what most people do not understand—and that is what deserves to be shouted from the rooftops.

Ironically, this connection between political and economic freedom is perfectly understood by totalitarians. *The communist theoretician knows precisely how to destroy individual freedom; he destroys economic freedom, and the job is done. More specifically, he expropriates private property, the means of production, and he forbids profits. He places the entire production-exchange-consumption chain under the direct rule of the state, which means, of course, that he places the physical life of each individual at the mercy of the state. That is the essence of tyranny.*

The totalitarian, of course, never announces that his intention is to enslave people. Quite the contrary, he invariably proposes to "liberate" them. He rationalizes his tyranny righteously in the name of the collective well-being of the "proletariat," "race," or "fatherland" or in the name of "public interest," "brotherhood," or "equality." But all these are invariably just rationalizations; the goal of tyranny is tyranny.

And inexorably it destroys economic life. The ultimate result is inevitably grinding poverty, an inability to produce.

The rulers of the Soviet Union are fully aware that they preside over a sick and stagnant economy, and they are also aware that they cannot go on indefinitely starving their own people and depriving them of the most modest amenities of life. At the same time, they know exactly how America generates its technological innovation and wealth. They know that only by decentralizing and individualizing the decision-making process and allowing free, competitive markets to develop across the length and breadth of the Soviet Union can they generate technology and wealth. But, as one observer has said, "To cure the patient would kill the doctor." To introduce true incentives and economic freedom into the Soviet Union would destroy the communist state.

These are the polar systems of political-economic organization: at one extreme, a free, unplanned, individualist market in a free individualist society which creates a powerful and inventive economic system and produces wealth; at the other, totalitarian-collectivist planning which destroys both the political and the economic freedom of the individual and produces collective poverty and starvation. Only when one has a good grasp of these polar alternatives is it possible to understand what has been going on—and going wrong—in Western countries, and in our own country in particular, in the past few decades.

To understand it, one need merely ask one question: What would happen to a society if someone tried to *mix* these contradictory polar systems in the life of a nation? What would happen if one tried to mix the free and the totalitarian, the unplanned and the planned, the individualist and the collectivist elements in economic life? For an answer, we must examine the industrialized nations of the West. Their economic "mix" is known by many names—"liberalism," "interventionism," "mixed economy," the "welfare state," "social democracy," "democratic socialism," even "socialism."

None of these terms has a precise definition, but societies with such economies share certain characteristics: Their intellectual and political leaders share the illusion that a comparative handful of individuals can substitute their judgment for the billions and trillions of decisions that go on in a free market. Generally, they believe it possible to use central planning to "correct" free market processes without destroying the market itself. They advocate planning to increase economic efficiency, to enforce competition, to eliminate the business cycle, to manipulate the money supply and rates of interest, to determine prices and profits, to redistribute property and income, to speed up or slow down the growth of the economy, to prevent discrimination, to eliminate pollution and several hundred other things. Whatever such gentlemen deem to be in need of improvement is sufficient cause for them to turn to central planning as a solution. The result of such political leadership is a system that was accurately described by *Newsweek* magazine (October 18, 1976) in an article entitled "Is Socialism in Trouble?" "By and large," the writer said, "social democracy seeks a middle ground between communism and capitalism."

The advocates of economic intervention clearly believe that their aims are worthy. But if one deflects one's attention from the meritorious motives and goals of such planners and simply looks at the nature of the system they have created—"a middle ground between communism and capitalism"—one sees that this is a regressive trend.

Few people would have any difficulty in understanding that if communist countries were to move in the direction of capitalism, that would be a decided sign of progress. If we were to hear, for example, that the Soviet Union was abandoning its centralized planning, opening up the nation to individual initiative and to free markets, most people would realize that totalitarianism was on the decline, that freedom was on the rise, that technological innovation and wealth could be expected to increase. But most of the same people cannot see that when a politically and economically free society starts to contract individual initiative, to contract the freedom of the market, political liberty is on the decline, inventiveness must decay, and wealth must decrease. Yet, if one really understands the polar systems, there is nothing particularly difficult about this calculation. A nation that decreases its economic freedom *must* be less politically free. And because freedom is a precondition for economic creativity and wealth, that nation *must* grow poorer. It follows as night follows day. *If* one understands the polar systems.

There are, of course, significant differences in the various mixes of freedom and coercive control in the Western countries. The nature, the degree, the rigidity, and the duration of the government's power over the economy; the number of areas affected; the momentum of the prior free economy—all these elements and many others will determine the nature, speed, and severity of the deterioration. As a result, I am in no position to account for all the various differences we see in the Western nations and for their different rates of deterioration. All I can do, like everyone else, is to observe some of these differences.

In Italy and France the trends are clear-cut: Both nations are drifting in the direction of totalitarianism. In Italy, where the dominant modern experience has been that of strong government controls, we see incessant economic disturbance, intransigent poverty, chaos, endless strikes, and the strong development of a communist movement. In France, where the prewar economy had been virtually calcified by government controls, the postwar "cure" once again was centralized planning. Again, such planning has resulted in economic chaos, strikes, riots, "revolutions" and in severe economic, political and social disturbance.

In both Italy and France a number of factors have both camouflaged and delayed the crisis—mainly the Marshall Plan and the enormous postwar injection of U.S. wealth into these economies, plus, of course, the surviving strength of their own increasingly hobbled markets. But it is now becoming apparent that both these nations are drifting, almost helplessly, toward communist economies. Needless to say, in both countries there is strong resistance to this trend in certain sectors. But it seems fairly certain that communists will now be a staple element in the political leadership of those countries and that political freedom itself is grossly threatened.

In West Germany the development has been strikingly different. National Socialism and war had reduced Germany to ashes. A brilliant Minister of Economic Affairs named Ludwig Erhard, who knew what he was doing, pulled West Germany out of collapse by the simple expedient of ·yanking out most government controls and letting a free economy rip. The result was an extraordinary laboratory demonstration of the relationship of a politically free economy and the production of wealth. Erhard launched a free enterprise Germany to the top of the list of productive nations in a few short years.

On the communist side of the Berlin Wall the poverty remained deadly. One might suppose that with such a comparative experiment going on under their noses, the West

Germans might have learned the value of a free, untrammeled economy. But they didn't. They turned back to government intervention and became a "social democracy." Their incredible growth has slowed considerably. And today, while Germany remains a powerful nation, few realize that its wealth and strength are a result of that massive productive momentum generated by the freedom given to the postwar market and by the resolve, even by a socialist government, to resist easy money and inflationary ruin.

In Sweden yet another variation on the theme has existed. For a variety of reasons an "advanced welfare state" has developed in Sweden and remained relatively stable for 44 years. The stability has been due in part to the gradual development of the Swedish social system, a slow, steady move in the direction of state control over individual life without traumatic swings between free market and severe regulation as in Germany. It has been due in part to the fact that those ambitious citizens who could not tolerate the growingly oppressive bureaucracy and the economic ceilings that menaced their goals simply left. In addition, there is a culturally and psychologically homogeneous working class which places immensely high value on economic security and economic equality and is relatively indifferent to competitive individual achievement. For these and other reasons the Swedish people on the whole have willingly accepted almost suffocating bureaucratic supervision of every detail of their lives—the state dictates the color a man may paint his house; he may chose from shades of *tan*!—in exchange for cradle-to-grave protection.

For this protection—exceeded nowhere on earth—the Swedes have been willing to pay an extraordinary percentage of their income. The average industrial worker pays $4125 in taxes on a salary of about $11,000. The most successful members of Swedish society, in business, the arts and all the independent professions, have as much as 85 percent of their income confiscated. Inevitably, signs of economic deterioration are present in Sweden. In 1976 a study by Hudson Research, Europe, showed that Sweden had the slowest growth rate of 14 industrialized nations—second only to that of Britain.

The United Kingdom offers yet another variation on the mixed economy theme. Economically wrecked after World War II, the U.K. did not emulate the wisdom of Germany's Ludwig Erhard, but moved in the opposite direction. To "cure" their society, they turned massively to socialist measures. Ralph Harris, director of the Institute of Economic Affairs in London, summarizes the results in a pungent phrase: The socialist leaders of Britain created a "progression from socialist planning to planned chaos." And the postwar "planned chaos" has simply grown worse. In 1975 Harris called British central planning a "total failure": "Cumulatively, since 1960, record levels of unemployment and inflation have come to exist with flagging growth and a sinking pound...."

No one predicted this tragic outcome more accurately than Winston Churchill. Ousted from office by the socialists in 1945, this eloquent statesman wrote:

"Personal initiative, competitive selection, the profit motive, corrected by failure and the infinite processes of good housekeeping and personal ingenuity, these constitute the life of a free society. It is this vital creative impulse that I deeply fear the doctrines and policies of the socialist government have destroyed.

"Nothing that they can plan and order and rush around enforcing will take its place. They have broken the mainspring, and until we get a new one, the watch will not go. Set the people free—get out of the way and let them make the best of themselves.

"I am sure that this policy of equalizing misery and organizing scarcity instead of allowing diligence, self-interest and ingenuity to produce abundance has only to be prolonged to kill this British island stone dead."

The British "planned economy" *is* "stone dead." It has survived to this day only by devouring the productivity of its citizens. The British now pay taxes that allow the government to confiscate 60 percent of the national income. A royal commission has reported that the *richest* one percent of the British populace earned more than $13,700—the same year that the *median* American income was $12,956. The most successful of the "rich"—those who earn more than $40,000 a year—lose an average of 83 percent of their income to the government. And profits—considered by Keynesian doctrinaires as socially noxious—are virtually confiscated; they are taxed at 98 percent! Inevitably throughout the decades there has been a leakage from Britain of the enterprising, the productive, the ambitious, and those intellectuals and artists who place a high value on their individual achievements, the same "brain drain" that has occurred in all "social democratic" countries. Physicians today are fleeing in great numbers because Labor policy seeks to eliminate what remains of private medicine and private hospital care. But above all, *capital* is leaking out of Britain to be invested abroad, where it will not be confiscated. There is no longer the slightest incentive for a Briton to invest his capital in British industry.

There are other case histories of comparable developments in mixed economies or "liberal" social democracies, but these are ample to make my point. Whatever the variations on the theme, those nations that have sought a genuine mix of the polar opposites of a free and an unfree economy, of the unplanned and the planned, of the individualist and the collectivist—of communism and capitalism—are slowly deteriorating or rapidly rotting, both socially and economically, and liberty itself is being corroded. And although in every one of those nations there is acute unease and anxiety over political trends, rare are the Europeans who fully understand why their worlds are running down or collapsing. All have been taught that the political directions in which they have moved constituted "progress"; all have been taught that the free market was an archaic and reactionary concept. And their "enlightened" reforms have led inexorably to shrinking profits, falling investment and plunging growth rates.

Many of these facts crossed my mind as I flew back from the Soviet Union. The speed of my plane made me think of the speed with which the disease has spread to the United States, where a younger, more vibrant nation, just into its third century, is itself degenerating into a social democracy. As compared to the European nations mentioned, the United States is apparently in the least amount of trouble. Our industrial sector, riding on the awesome momentum of more than two centuries of freedom, is still, for all the intervention and regulation, breathtakingly inventive and rich. And in worldwide terms we can still describe ourselves as a free enterprise or free market economy. But today these terms have only a relative meaning. In the context of our own past and by the standards of our once exceptionally free market, we have ceased to be a true free enterprise economy, and we are today a mixed economy or "welfare state."

Despite our comparative wealth, our situation is unusually ominous, for cultural, as well as economic, reasons. In the United States a population accustomed to historically unprecedented liberty is now ruled, almost exclusively, by a political-social-intellectual elite that is committed to the belief that government can control our complex marketplace by fiat better than the people can by individual choice. They believe, tragically, that one can drastically mix polar political opposites, that one can fuse the dynamics of "communism and capitalism" within one society.

Our political leadership today articulates a philosophy of individualism and collectivism, of the free market and a planned economy, of individual liberty from government coercion and of government control over individual life. The American political language has become paralyzed by these conflicting assignments. It is impossible to articulate such massively contradictory "ideals." And those politicians who attempt to resolve this problem end up speaking a mediocre kind of double talk so rife with self-contradiction that they are winning the contempt of millions of Americans.

There is a reason for our leaders' special degree of incoherence and confusion. The United States, in changing with relative speed into a social democracy, has undergone an alteration that is more fundamental than any other nation's. It has actually repudiated its own *identity*. America was born a capitalist nation; was created a capitalist nation by the intent of its founders and the Constitution. An American who is hostile to individualism, to the work ethic, to free enterprise, who advocates an increasing government takeover of the economy or who advocates the coercive socialization of American life is in some profound sense advocating that America cease being America. He is advocating values that are not American and are philosophically antithetical to America itself.

What is happening in this country is a fundamental assault on America's culture and its historic identity. Before he died a few years ago, Arthur Krock, the retired Washington bureau chief of the New York *Times*, wrote in his memoirs: "... the U.S. merits the dubious distinction of having discarded its past and its meaning in one of the briefest spans of modern history."

It is not surprising, in this situation, that our political leaders should become virtually incoherent and unable to articulate the ideals of this nation and that our public should become confused and suffer from a crisis of distrust in its leadership. Nothing else could really have been expected once the ideals themselves were repudiated by the "enlightened" with contempt and with hatred.

It is widely sensed that a "mysterious" malady is eating away at the core of our society, but we are drowning in shallow explanations. Yet the reason is plain. The "mysterious" malady is that the freest land in the world is becoming unfree, that America's unique historical attributes—the brilliant interlocking of political liberty and economic liberty—are slowly being destroyed.

III

Dictatorship in Microcosm

> We've always had a finite amount of energy.... We had finite supplies of wood in the early pioneer days. How did we make the transition from using wood to using coal, from using coal to using oil, from using oil to using natural gas? How in God's name did we make that transition without a Federal Energy Agency?
>
> —MILTON FRIEDMAN

In December 1973 I myself became an illustration of a free-market principle—the very one that allowed Winston Churchill to predict the disastrous outcome of the British welfare state decades in advance. That principle states that government planning and regulation of the economy will ultimately lead to shortages, crises, and, if not reversed in time, some form of economic dictatorship. That is precisely what happened in the realm of energy production in the United States. Years of incoherent government intervention strangled energy production, domestic supplies diminished, artificial shortages emerged, a foreign embargo on oil precipitated a crisis, there was a violent public outcry for an instant solution, an energy "dictatorship" was established to allocate the rare commodity—and I, incredibly, became the "dictator."

The American energy crisis is a classic case out of a free-market textbook, and for that reason I shall describe it in detail because unless one sees the planning and regulatory system close up, it is difficult to resist the entrancing notion that conscious planning by the state is a reasonable process.

On December 4, 1973, with the nation reeling under the Arab

17

oil embargo, President Nixon named me energy czar, the American euphemism for a mini-dictator over a portion of the economy. *There is nothing like becoming an economic planner oneself to learn what is desperately, stupidly wrong with such a system.*

Needless to say, I did not acquire that strange role overnight. I passed through an apprenticeship of sorts. It began immediately after I was named Deputy Secretary of the Treasury under George Shultz. I arrived at the Treasury in November 1972, and I was boning up on financial matters, law enforcement, and the various international issues in which Treasury is involved when I was summoned one evening by Shultz. He told me that he and the President had decided to make me chairman of the Oil Policy Committee. I was astonished and replied, "But I don't know a thing about oil." Shultz said, "That's all right. You'll learn."

No sooner did the rumor get out that I was to chair the Oil Policy Committee than I was deluged by advice, demands and warnings from an incredible number of interested parties, ranging from the 55 federal agencies which had been regulating the oil industry, to the industry itself—the major companies and the independents, marketers, producers, refiners and jobbers. The assault was dizzying.

To learn everything I could about energy, I set up the equivalent of a school for myself. I chose as my "professors" the men who had impressed me most strongly as knowing what they were talking about: James Akins of the State Department, who was soon to become the ambassador to Saudi Arabia; Peter Flanigan of the White House; Stephen Wakefield of the Department of the Interior; and Duke Ligon and William Johnson, energy advisers in the Treasury Department. And for three months—for up to five hours a day, almost every evening and solidly through weekends—they educated me on energy in general, oil in particular, the mandatory import quota policy, and the international implications of all the issues involved. By the end of the three-month period, in the spring of 1973, I had received from these gentlemen the equivalent of a master's degree on the subject of energy.

I had worked with such fervor because I was determined to assist the Nixon administration to achieve its goal: energy independence. In both 1971 and 1973 President Nixon had sent energy messages to Congress to that effect. He wanted the deregulation of natural gas and the simplification of various regulatory procedures that were greatly delaying energy development. The more I learned about the energy problems of the nation, the more certain I became that there were few more important things on the agenda. I was shocked to learn the degree to which our energy industries were stagnating and struggling futilely against regulatory shackles. In the oil realm, demand was rising constantly; but domestic exploration and production were declining sharply, and from year to year we were growing more dependent on imports. All the elements of an impending energy catastrophe were visible.

Then, without warning, the unthinkable happened. In October 1973, in the wake of the Yom Kippur War, the Arab countries unanimously decided to place an embargo on their oil sales. Suddenly America had no access to imported Arab oil. The long-dreaded energy crisis had arrived. And I became energy czar.

The first problem I faced was an explosion of political mythology which denied the very reality of the oil shortage. Thanks to a press which emphasizes the minutiae of the day and supplies few, if any, of the connective links, the American public had never learned adequately about the dangerous decline in oil and gas exploration—all caused by shortsighted policies—and the consequent rise in our dependence on foreign oil imports. I had testified repeatedly about it before Congress, usually in the presence of the press. But those sections of my testimonies were rarely covered. Few people realized that before the embargo we had been importing one-third of our oil—6.5 million barrels a day out of a total of more than 17 million barrels used. Of these 6.5 million, about 2.7 million came directly or indirectly from the Middle East. Thus, the embargo left a shocking hole in our economy.

This reality could not be contested save by the ignorant, and the voice of ignorance was heard in the land, churning out accusations that the shortage had been contrived by the oil companies to get higher prices, that thousands of tankers were lingering offshore until the prices rose. These charges surged through the network news mechanisms and flooded the country with paranoid suspicions. I spent a ludicrous amount of time simply struggling to convince people that the crisis was real.

Even many of those who acknowledge the reality of the crisis were gripped by the equally mythical belief that a rigid program of gasoline rationing could solve the problem. It was an idea I opposed with every ounce of strength. So, to his great credit, did President Nixon, who knew that rationing would wreak havoc with the market and would be a bureaucratic nightmare.

As for the centralized allocation process itself, the kindest thing I can say about it is that it was a disaster. Even with a stack of sensible-sounding plans for even-handed allocation all over the country, the system kept falling apart, and chunks of the populace suddenly found themselves without gas. There was no logic to the pattern of failures. In Palm Beach suddenly there was no gas, while ten miles away gas was plentiful. Parts of New Jersey suddenly went dry, while other parts of New Jersey were well supplied. Every day, in different parts of the country, people waited in line for gasoline for two, three, and four hours. The normal market distribution system is so complex, yet so smooth that no government mechanism could simulate it. All we were actually doing with our so-called bureaucratic efficiency was damaging the existent distribution system.

Toward the end of January I told my bureaucracy in the Allocation Center that I wanted additional allocations from our reserves sent to all the pockets of shortages in the country to break the gas lines and stop the hysteria. The bureaucracy was appalled. "You can't do that," I was told. "Why not?" I demanded. "Because six or more months from now, when midsummer comes and the demand is at its greatest, we will have no reserves." I understood the risk, but I also understood *when* to take a risk. The hysterical buying and hoarding had to be stopped. We worked out allocations, sent the forms over to the FEO, and I ordered that they sign them. Within 36 hours the gas lines were cracked. The embargo lasted another six weeks, but the fever had been taken out of the public response. As far as I was concerned and as far as the American gas buyer was concerned, the emergency had been handled successfully.

That was by no means the assessment of the Washington bureaucracy, however, which poured its protests into the press. On March 22 the Federal Trade Commission staff, after a study of the FEO, wrote: "By most tests of administrative effectiveness, FEO has been found wanting and increasingly so as the problems to be dealt with grow in severity." In sum, I was charged with being a rotten bureaucrat, and by their standards I *was* a rotten bureaucrat. In fact, I was worse than that. I was an *anti*bureaucrat. I ignored most of my bureaucracy and worked with only a handful of brilliant, mostly non-Civil Service staffers. I could discover no other way to accomplish anything. In the crunch I had used the decisive methods that had served me well in the marketplace.

That is how I ultimately realized the profundity of the difference between the businessman and the government bureaucrat. The businessman's standard of efficacy is a solution to the problem, and the more responsive he is to external reality, the better. *The bureaucrat's standard of efficacy is obedience to the rules and respect for the vested interests of the hierarchy, however unyielding of a solution. That is why bureaucracies so often produce nothing but wastepaper and destroy the productive institutions they supervise. Bureaucrats are actually the first victims of their own regulations, the primary effect of which is to inhibit individual thought and the courage to take responsibility.*

While I was playing the philosophically preposterous role of William E. Simon, Invisible Hand, I got my first insight into the extraordinary irresponsibility of that collection of economic planners known as Congress, particularly the compulsion to believe any rumor, however baseless, from any source, however absurd, which suggested that the shortage was "unreal," a product of a vicious oil company plot.

This compulsion was itself Congress' most damaging contribution to the energy crisis simply because it kept most legislators from understanding the actual causes of the crisis, which in turn rendered them incapable of projecting rational solutions. To get a perspective on the immensity of this self-blinding, one must have a more detailed understanding of the causes which had been incessantly explained to Congress over a period of two decades. I have broken them down here in simple form so that they can be readily grasped.

1. Congress had been repeatedly told that there was no shortage of fuel as such. The known sources of fossil fuels are abundant, and we have barely begun to explore vast areas of the United States, including Alaska, the offshore resources or the sea. Only in terms of what we have *already* discovered, not of the vast unknown potentials, the facts are these:

COAL.

We have half of all the coal reserves in the noncommunist world, of which at least 425 billion tons are immediately recoverable. At 1973 levels of consumption we have enough coal for 800 years.

NATURAL GAS.

We have potential natural gas reserves of 920 trillion cubic feet, according to the U.S. Geological Survey—enough for 40 to 50 years at 1972 rates of consumption.

OIL.

There are an estimated 50 to 127 billion barrels of oil still untapped in continental America, according to the U.S. Geological Survey. In addition, we have proved resources of 40.6 billion barrels, despite the fact that we have explored by drilling only four percent of the Outer Continental Shelf.

NUCLEAR.

We are the world's technological pioneers in nuclear energy production, which, in its various forms, can yield limitless energy.

2. Congress had been repeatedly told that despite those great potential fuel reserves, not to mention the vast unexplored areas, production had been severely inhibited.

COAL.

Our coal production today is barely more than it was 30 years ago. In 1960 coal represented 23 percent of our energy consumption. By 1974 it had dropped to 18 percent.

NATURAL GAS.

Since 1968 our gas production has been steadily shrinking. By 1973 new reserve additions were less than one-third of consumption, and the nation's total natural gas reserves dropped from a 15-year supply in 1967 to a less-than-ten-year reserve.

OIL.

There has been a steady decline in the number of oil wells drilled in the United States. Between 1955 and 1972 the number dropped from 31,567 to 11,306 a year. Additionally, construction of new refineries in this country has come to a standstill.

NUCLEAR.

After 30 years of development, nuclear energy in 1975 was supplying only two percent of our energy needs, with Germany, France, and Japan systematically outpacing us in construction of nuclear plants,

3. Congress had been repeatedly told that various laws and regulations were primarily responsible for this inhibition of exploration and production in all energy realms.

COAL.

In 1969 and 1970 the Coal Mining Health and Safety Act and the Clean Air Act were passed. The latter forbids the burning of high-sulfur coal, the most readily accessible, unless it is first cleaned in scrubbers, which are exceedingly costly and in many cases technologically infeasible. The immediate result of both laws: Coal production crashed 30 percent. The problem was compounded by the Congressional attempt to pass legislation restricting surface strip mining of coal. The likelihood that such legislation would be signed into law effectively prevented the development of massive quantities of our low-sulfur Western coal.*

NATURAL GAS.

In 1954 the Supreme Court clamped a complex system of price controls on all natural gas sold for transmission in interstate commerce. Incentives for industry to spend billions of dollars developing new supplies and technologies and exploring the methane-rich waters along the Gulf Coast were all but destroyed by the artificially low prices that followed. By the late 1960s shortages had developed throughout the nation except in the non-price-controlled intrastate gas-producing areas.

OIL.

A system of quotas instituted in 1959 restricted the importation of crude oil but encouraged the importation of refined products. Thus, construction of refineries in this country slowed to a standstill, and when President Nixon announced his goals of Project Independence, there was insufficient capacity to make possible the shift to domestic crude oil sources. In 1973 Nixon was able to scrap the mandatory quota system—as I had

---

*Such legislation was signed into law by President Carter on August 3, 1977.

urged—but the damage had been done over the previous 14 years.

In addition, environmental restrictions blocked exploration and drilling, prompted further stagnation in the building of refineries, and led inevitably to soaring costs. In 1969 Congress passed the National Environmental Policy Act, which requires that "environmental impact" studies be prepared by the Department of the Interior and reviewed by Congress before any drilling or construction can be done. The act allowed environmental groups to block every stage of the proceedings. Since that law was passed, it takes three to five years to obtain site approval alone and a similar period for construction, not to mention the time spent meeting the incessant lawsuits by environmental groups. Oil companies started to leave the country; it had become simpler and cheaper to set up refineries in the Caribbean and in Canada.

To cap all this, the record of deliberate strangulation of the thousands of companies that make up our oil industry can be matched in idiocy only by the simultaneous record of financial indulgence to the oil companies. With the left hand the U.S. government paralyzed their operations, and with the right hand it granted them absurd tax exemptions and a variety of subsidies "to stimulate incentive"—an incentive which the government itself had done its utmost to destroy.

The result of all this, in a magnificently energy-rich and technologically superior nation, is that the United States paid the OPEC oil cartel more than $40 billion in 1977 versus $2.7 billion in 1970. And each year our dependency on imported oil grows, our dollars continue to flow to the OPEC nations rather than to our own domestic companies and workers—and the national security is further threatened.

NUCLEAR.

A crazy quilt of environmental regulations has so inhibited the creation of nuclear power plants that it now takes as much as 11 years to build such a plant, almost three times as long as it takes in Europe and Japan. The costs of such prolongation of the building process are such that they are destroying economic incentive and driving the price of nuclear energy to noncompetitive levels. Already major and experienced firms are leaving the nuclear energy industry. In Europe, by contrast, the building period is only from four to four and one half years, with the consequence that the nuclear industry is growing steadily—and safely—despite the opposition of European environmentalists.*

For years, Congress has been told that we are on a collision course with reality, that shortsighted, politically expedient policies are denying us the energy we need to survive and jeopardizing our very future. But Congress has proved incapable of grasping these simple facts or of seeing its own ludicrous culpability in the matter. The reason for the Congressional blindness is clear. The very regulatory philosophy that has chopped prices, jacked up costs and outlawed fuel production represents the highest liberal "good." Men cannot perceive their "good" as the source of evil, and the liberals are no exception.

Thus, the liberal hue and cry in the course of the energy crisis were precisely what one would expect. Liberals on the whole perceived no fault in government and tried to interpret events in terms of the few facts that were left when one omitted the government's destructive role. Many perceived the shortages as the end of energy sources and began to emit apocalyptic shrieks. Modern man had greedily plundered the earth, they cried, warning that Americans must immediately return to a life of simplicity. Primitivism became a fad in the trendy upper middle class; the well-to-do took to eating alfalfa sprouts and growing organic tomatoes on high-rise terraces. Leftist ideologues

---

*I am aware, incidentally, that my reliance on the insurance policy of nuclear energy flies in the face of the revealed wisdom of the environmentalist, consumerist and public interest factions led by Ralph Nader, which have ceaselessly sought to ban nuclear energy production as "unsafe." They do entail risks as, for that matter, do all forms of energy production. One of the most important functions of technological development is to diminish those risks. But the various Naderite factions seem incapable of differentiating between the type of risk that may affect a tiny fraction of the population and the certain destruction of an entire civilization that would result from paralyzing energy production.

I am vastly more impressed with the wisdom of Hans Bethe, that giant of theoretical physics who helped discover nuclear fission. Bethe and several hundred other physicists of great national and international repute, including many Nobel Prize winners, are fighting to save nuclear energy production in this country from the Naderites and the major media, which serve as their press agents. They are well aware of the risks entailed in nuclear production, and they consider it remarkably safe—safer, in fact, than all other types of energy production. What's more, the national and international safety record of the past 20 years of nuclear energy production bears them out.

eagerly recited their cherished myth that "capitalism was in its final crisis."

In time, such men as Sen. Edward Brooke of Massachusetts and Sen. John Tunney of California finally grasped the fact that price controls were choking the production of natural gas. In 1975 they jointly launched a recommendation that "new" onshore natural gas be deregulated. Congress in general, however, had not achieved even this minimal insight and deregulated nothing.

By 1976 the terrain for hatcheting the oil companies to bits had been prepared. In June the Senate Judiciary Committee approved by an eight-to-seven vote a bill sponsored by Sen. Birch Bayh called the Petroleum Industry Competition Act. It proposed the breakup of 18 of the nation's largest oil companies into separate production, refining, transportation, and marketing entities on the grounds that they constituted a monopoly. But the charge had no rational base. As of 1976, there were 8000 different oil and gas producers, 130 refiners and 16,000 wholesale marketers—to say nothing of 186,000 service stations, the vast majority of which were run by independent businessmen. And this was a monopoly? One of the most thorough examinations of the industry on record—a collection of analyses called "Vertical Integration in the Oil Industry," edited by Professor Edward J. Mitchell of the University of Michigan—demonstrates that none of the characteristics of monopolies are present in that industry.

The oil industry fought bitterly against the proposed divestiture legislation, and its widely circulated arguments won considerable acceptance. More than 250 newspapers, including the Washington *Post*, took strong antidivestiture stands. The anti-oil Congressmen discovered that they would lose, so rather than let the oil companies win a victory, they quietly put the bill on ice.

Essentially the same blindness to fact has been present in the uproar over the oil companies' "obscene profits." That charge too is baseless and equally easy to disprove.

It is true that after the OPEC embargo hit, oil profits did reach a historic high. The sudden shortage, followed immediately by OPEC's 300 percent price increase, drove domestic prices up. The result: a recorded leap of 81.5 percent over the profits registered at the same period the year before, which, incidentally, was the worst profit year in nearly two decades. But there is something bizarre about people who see in this statistic a cause of battle but remain indifferent to far greater profit leaps in other industries. During the same quarter, compared to the year before, metalworking machinery and equipment profits rose by 700 percent, almost nine times the oil leap. Oil, in fact, ranked seventh in a group of industries whose profits surged ahead in that period, but the liberals in Congress screamed only about oil.

And even that does not adequately reveal the magnitude of their selective perception. In 1974 the Treasury Department did a study of the profits of the 19 biggest oil companies, based on data collected by the FTC, as compared to other industries. Between 1958 and 1973 the petroleum industry ranked in the middle range of the 29 industries studied.

My education in the energy realm was not complete until I truly understood the nature of the oil hysteria of the liberal Democrats. It is a symbolic mania sheltered by a profound refusal to look at the facts. Such writers and journalists as Theodore White, Irving Kristol, Howard K. Smith, and the late Stewart Alsop have observed that their liberal brethren were out of contact with reality, trapped in a maze of preconceived notions. That maze, I realized, is the liberal ideology itself—a hash of statism, collectivism, egalitarianism, and anticapitalism, mixed with the desire for the *results* of capitalism.

Too many Americans have assumed immense intelligence in the liberal world and have concluded that when liberals destroyed U.S. production, they knew what they were doing— i.e., that they were guilty of a conspiracy. They are not conspirators; they are intellectual basket cases in the realm of basic economics. Amy Carter could understand perfectly well what was wrong if her father "regulated" her lemonade stand the way the liberals in Congress have regulated the energy industry. Unfortunately her father, who made his money in a regulated, subsidized industry, does not understand it.

Strangely enough it was not until I understood the liberals, who dominate our political life, that I was finally able to understand my own fellow Republicans, with whom I have been on a restless four-year journey. A friend of mine once wisecracked, "A Republican is a Democrat who knows he's crazy." And there is truth to his claim. Too often, the Republican tends to buck but ultimately follows Democratic trends. Unlike the Democrat, however, he commits his economic misdeeds in a state of moral depression and is not in the slightest astonished when the disasters occur because he always knew they would.

If Republicans know anything at all, they know what is involved in the production of wealth. Thus, the intelligent Republican free enterpriser knows exactly how to solve the energy crisis. He knows he should deregulate the tortured productive system; drop price controls, destructive bans, and crippling subsidies; and let exploration and production rip with the profit motive as guide, allowing prices to find their true market level. And then, when the United States is roaring with energy production and vice-presidents in charge of research and development are poring over innovative technologies to release yet other forms of energy, he should go off to play a healthy round of golf. That is the Republican at his best and at his most useful to the nation.

But for 40 years those free enterprise values that made America a lusty, inventive giant have been discredited. And after decades of functioning as a minority in a philosophically inimical atmosphere, the Republican—with notable exceptions—has lost his moorings. To survive politically, he has often felt obligated to modify, compromise, abandon and betray many of his own standards. Most of the time he has no hope of being able to do what he thinks is right. So he frequently does what he thinks is half right or wrong or even god-awful. He floats trial balloons to see if he can sneak through something economically sane, but if they fail, he scuttles quickly to safety, which means an imitation Democratic position. Since this is, in fact, a shameful way of life, he has devised certain standard rationalizations for it. One of the most frequent is: "If *we* don't propose or accept some bad legislation, the Democrats will propose worse." And this is usually followed by the corollary: "So long as that legislation is in *our* hands, *we* won't damage the country or the free enterprise system the way *they* would."

I witnessed the precise enactment of this little drama one day when, as Secretary of the Treasury, I was no longer in charge of energy policy. I got a phone call from a reporter for the *Wall Street Journal*, who asked, "What do you think about extending the life of the Federal Energy Administration?" The FEA was supposed to go out of business after the emergency but had lingered on to proliferate, malignantly. The thought that it was being further extended horrified me. I exclaimed, "Extend its life! That place is a menace. It's strangling the energy industry at the very time when we need production. It should be wiped out of existence." My views appeared in the next day's *Journal*. But that same day I learned that President Ford had already decided to extend the life of this bureaucratic abortion.

I went charging over to the 8 a.m. White House meeting with blood in my eye, and there I heard the classical Republican rationalization from my very close friend Frank Zarb, the FEA director. "At least we're keeping all the garbage in one place so *we* can control it rather than distribute it all over government." I answered, "You've forgotten one thing. One day *you're* not going to be here, but *that horrible thing* is still going to be here." And the chief economic counselors to President Ford—Alan Greenspan, Paul MacAvoy and Paul O'Neill—all spoke almost simultaneously and said, "Yes, get *rid* of the damned thing." But it was too late.

The last Republican rationalization for betraying free enterprise is a time-honored one: "It's necessary to stay in power. We can accomplish nothing if we're out of office. So we have to throw the voters the kinds of bones to which the Democrats have accustomed them." A man who uses this rationalization so frequently that he believes it is known as a progressive Republican. President Ford, a conservative, didn't believe it. He just used it on occasion. And the fearful result was his acceptance of the Energy Policy and Conservation Act of 1975. One of the provisions—the one emphasized by the press—was the promise to give voters cheaper energy. After long years of battling for a sensible energy policy, Ford caved in. Anxious for a quick political fix just before the New Hampshire and Florida primaries, he signed the bill.

The EPCA was, in my judgment, the worst error of the Ford administration, which started out bravely enough. The President vetoed shortsighted strip mining legislation that would have cut back on desperately needed coal production. He pressed for expanded oil production in the frontier areas of Alaska and the Outer Continental Shelf. He sought to remove the regulatory roadblocks that were crippling the nuclear industry and to guarantee that by 1986, 300 nuclear plants would be supplying 20 percent of the nation's electricity. Finally, the President recommended the immediate lifting of all price controls from oil and natural gas since it is impossible to have increased exploration, production, and innovative technology when the government holds the price artificially below the market price. But the Democrats resisted. And with each round of resistance Ford cut down his own proposal, prolonged the price control period, until by about the third round of compromises, he was accepting a 40-month extension of price controls and other provisions virtually identical to those in a bill he had vetoed a year earlier. The President finally ended up agreeing to *more complex* price controls on *more* oil than had ever existed before. His subsequent pleas that Congress deregulate natural gas were simply ignored, and the nation was saddled with a disastrous energy law.

That Republicans who claim to be dedicated to free enterprise and to the welfare of this nation should have cooperated in the framing of this bill and that a Republican President should have signed it are tragic. In this life there are issues on which men may reasonably compromise, and there are issues over which one must fight, even if one goes down in flames. As far as I am concerned, energy production, the vital life-force of the United States, is an issue over which one must fight.

Thus, the Energy Policy and Conservation Act became law. It did not, of course, assure Gerald Ford's election the following November. With the inauguration of Jimmy Carter we all went back to our various homes, and I proceeded to work on this book. And while this book was being written, we had our next energy crisis—a frightening shortage of natural gas in the coldest winter in 100 years. Natural gas was concentrated, of course, in those states where the free market price existed and ran short in those states where federal price controls had reduced the supply. According to the press, about 10,000 factories, deprived of energy, closed. More than 1.5 million people were hurled into the deadly winter to stand on unemployment lines.

Had anything been learned at all? For a moment, yes. Some politicians understood this time that the solution was to run as fast as their legs would carry them to rip the price controls off the interstate transmission of natural gas—at least temporarily. Even some of the press grasped this. The *New York Times* and CBS, for example, explained the effect of those price controls on the natural gas supply clearly and accurately.

But many in the liberal world learned nothing at all. I watched, disbelievingly, the idiotic replay of all the events I have described in this chapter. Once again liberal voices exploded hysterically that the shortage was "unreal," contrived by natural gas companies to rip off the public. Congressmen bayed righteously at the scandalous refusal of American industrialists to produce at prices lower than their costs.

In April 1977 the Carter administration committed itself formally to the idea that only centralized planning by the state could solve the nation's energy problems. The legal base had been prepared by the Energy Policy and Conservation Act of 1975 and by another horrendous piece of legislation—the Energy Conservation and Production Act—which was authored by Sen. Edward Kennedy and signed into law by President Ford during the 1976 campaign. All the new administration had to do was to elaborate on the provisions of the two statutes, and Carter did just that. Focusing almost entirely on conservation, Carter proposed to restrict the use of energy by a complex design of taxes which, if enacted, would paralyze incentives in the energy industries. Specifically, they would make it impossible for our energy producers to earn the profits needed (1) to explore the vast areas of the earth and ocean that have not yet been investigated; (2) to extract what may be a 1000-year supply of gas in the Gulf of Mexico; (3) to extract an estimated 50 to 100 billion barrels of oil in Alaska; (4) to devise the new technology needed to recover 105 billion barrels in existing oil fields and to recover possibly two trillion barrels in U.S. oil shale deposits.

In addition, Carter sought to ban America's single most reliable long-range energy insurance policy, the liquid metal fast-breeder reactor. By that action, the Administration was actually refusing to use 200,000 tons of uranium 238 that are now being stored in steel boxes at Oak Ridge, Tenn., and elsewhere—the depleted uranium that remains after its fissionable isotope U-235 has been extracted. Petr Beckmann, professor of electrical engineering at the University of Colorado and editor of *Access to Energy*, clearly explained the meaning of that refusal: "The total amount of energy available from these reserves represents a staggering 140,000 quads, or about 1750 years of energy at the present rate of U.S. consumption."

What, indeed, did Carter offer the nation? He proposed a giant bureaucracy which would control every aspect of pricing, production, and consumption, not only in the energy-producing industries themselves but also in all industries that use energy or produce machines that use energy—automobiles, refrigerators, stoves, air conditioners. The tentacles of the proposed bureaucracy would reach into every home, office and factory in the land. *In effect, with that program Carter was advocating the effective nationalization of American industry, a strangling economic dictatorship. I described it publicly as a call for an "energy police state," and that is exactly what it was.*

The Carter program, like the energy legislation that preceded it, is a dramatic illustration of the principle with which I began this chapter: Government control of production results in artificial shortages which produce crises, and if not corrected, it will culminate in a drive to economic dictatorship. The principle is inviolate. Our capacity for innovation must decay, our standard of living must drop, and our wealth and freedom—and the wealth and freedom of those nations which depend on us—must deteriorate until the principle is finally understood.

IV

Disaster: Visible and Invisible

> The problem of the managed economy is like the
> problem of the waves of the sea. We have
> identified the forces that cause them, we appre-
> hend the conditions which must be met for a
> solution of the problem, and we can even reduce it
> to an equation—but its solution is hopelessly
> beyond our capacities.
>
> —JACQUES RUEFF

In April 1974 President Nixon named me Secretary of the
Treasury. The press of the period described the appointment as
"noncontroversial." That didn't last for I had resolved to fight
for the free enterprise system. And shout, "Stop!" to bigger and
bigger government.

As my intentions and determination became apparent, I was
warned by friends and associates that I could expect substantial
animosity from the liberal press, which was given to a primitive
cartooning of politicians as "good" and "evil"—with free
enterprisers being cast in the "evil" role. They were right. But
while reports were busily denouncing me in the name of the
"social democratic" mythology, I was making the most
important discoveries of my life, discoveries I knew to be of
long-range importance to the country.

As Secretary of the Treasury I could see the entire picture of
what was going on in the economy at every level. The experience
was shattering. It was very much like being a physician staring at
a wall full of X-rays and a stack of sophisticated test results and
realizing that the patient was not just sick but that every vital
organ was threatened. Add one fact—that the physician loved

34

the patient—and you have my state of mind in viewing the American economic condition.

Here are some of those "X-rays" and "test results." I have selected only those that a layman with no education in economics should be able to understand.

TAXES.

Washington was taking about one quarter of the national income. That meant in effect that we all would be working from January 1 to the end of March only to turn our total income over to the federal government; in addition, we would be working through April into early May only to turn our total income over to the state and local governments. On an average, more than four months out of every citizen's year of labor were being confiscated by the government.

The share of the Gross National Product eaten up by government had been inflating feverishly. In 1930 spending by federal, state and local governments accounted for 12 percent of the GNP. By 1976 it was 36 percent. If the trend continued, it would hit 60 percent by the year 2000.

GOVERNMENT SPENDING.

Federal spending had flown out of control. It had increased 232 percent from 1961 to 1975. The federal government was spending more than $1 billion a day. State and local spending had mushroomed 520 percent.

Government at all levels had become the nation's biggest employer, bigger than the auto, steel, and all other durable-goods manufacturers combined. One out of every six working people was employed by a federal, state, or local government.

In 1960 federal, state, and local governments spent a total of $52 billion on assorted social welfare programs. After Congress passed the Economic Opportunity Act in 1965, expenditures soared, rising over the next decade from $77.2 billion to a staggering total of $286 billion in 1975.

GOVERNMENT DEBT.

The U.S. government was in hock up to its ears. This catastrophe had taken decades to develop. Before the New Deal the American government had kept its federal budget in surplus for four years out of almost every five. Since the New Deal the federal budget had been in the red in nearly four years out of every five. In 16 of the past 17 years we had rolled up deficits. From 1965 to 1975 the national debt had soared from $313 billion to $533 billion.

The governmental statement of the federal debt was grossly deceptive. Enormous liabilities were not listed on the budget at all but were described as off-budget items. By 1975 $11 billion was owed by "independent" agencies like the TVA and the Export-Import Bank. Government-sponsored enterprises, such as the Farm Credit Administration and the Federal Home Loan Board, owed $88 billion. Loans totaling $237 billion were guaranteed by the Federal Housing Administration and others. But the biggest and still growing obligation was Social Security, estimated at more than $4 trillion—a figure which did not include Civil Service and other pensions.

REGULATORY AGENCIES.

Although the President's Council of Economic Advisers estimated in 1975 that regulation cost the citizens $130 billion a year, no one knew how to calculate precisely either the inhibitory or inflationary effects of these agencies. They exercised control over every aspect of the operations not only of interstate transportation, power generation, the securities market, electronic communications and the maritime, automobile, drug, food, agriculture and defense industries but of small business as well.

In 1974 General Motors reported that it cost them $1.3 billion to comply with government regulations—costs that were, of course, passed on to the consumer. The Interstate Commerce Commission had on its books about 400,000 tariff schedules and 40 trillion rates telling the transportation industry what it might charge customers. An estimated 130 million man-hours were being spent filling out bureaucratic forms at a cost of at least $25 billion, that sum being added to the basic price of America's goods and services. And government processing of that paperwork cost taxpayers a minimum of $15 billion more.

INFLATION.

To pay for both budget and off-budget items, as well as interest on the debt, the government was printing more money every year. From 1955 through 1965 the money supply had grown at an annual rate of 2½ percent. Since 1965 the money growth rate had averaged nearly six percent.

Prices had been soaring since the mid-1960s. From 1960 to 1964 inflation had averaged 1.2 percent a year. Then, from 1965 through 1968, the inflation rate doubled to 2.5 percent a year. In the next three years it doubled again, to more than five percent a year. The politically inspired imposition of wage and price controls artificially blocked inflation for the next two years. But when the controls were removed in 1973–74, inflation soared to more than 12 percent—the highest figure in our peacetime history.

PROFITS.

Since the mid-1960s, under the impact of rising taxes, inflation, redistribution of wealth programs and proliferating regulation, profits after taxes had been plummeting throughout the business world by every standard measurement used by economists. In ten years the actual profits made on every dollar of sales had plunged by 50 percent—from ten cents to less than five cents.

CAPITAL INVESTMENT.

The government was usurping funds needed for private investment. Approximately 70 percent of the long-term capital funds available in private money markets was being borrowed by the federal government and 80 percent by government at all levels. Capital investment was falling far short of that required for long-overdue plant expansion and technological innovation. From 1960 through the early 1970s private investment in the United States averaged less than 18 percent a year of our GNP. Capital investment in the United States was the lowest among all industrialized nations, including the United Kingdom. Productivity growth—heavily influenced by investment in new plants, equipment, and technology—was declining rapidly. Since 1960, of eight major industrialized nations, the United States has ranked last in productivity growth.

UNEMPLOYMENT.

In 1974–75 all these destructive trends came together, and the situation was worsened by several onetime factors, like the quadrupling of oil prices by the OPEC nations. The result was the worst inflation and recession in this country's history save for the Great Depression of 1929. Production declined drastically in many industries. Millions of people lost their jobs, and the unemployment rate hit nine percent.

Those are the "symptoms" I was looking at as Secretary of the Treasury. I have left out hundreds of others of a more technical nature, but all of them added up to only one thing: a government-engendered dynamics which was set *against* productive citizens, set *against* productivity, and set *against* the productive system. To all intents and purposes, a "stop growth" pattern had been built into the economic structure by the state itself.

What had brought the United States to such an impasse? There are a great many ways to explain it, but the simplest, by far, is to give you two kinds of explanations—one dominantly economic, the other dominantly philosophical and political. In effect, I will first explain the visible crisis and next the invisible. They can best be understood by reviewing them in the context of the four major government policies that caused them. Those policies were deficit spending, inflation of the money supply, regulatory policy, and wage and price controls.

DEFICIT SPENDING.

The inflationary cycle began, as all such cycles begin, with the extensive stimulus of government fiscal policies. For years American political leaders had been buying their way into power by promising to pay for and solve every problem, real or imaginary, domestic or foreign, that was declared by any sufficiently vocal and influential group to exist. Partisan versions of history notwithstanding, the malady was of both Democratic and Republican parentage.

By the time Lyndon Johnson's Great Society was in full swing in fiscal year 1966 federal outlays had reached $135 billion. Eight years later, under Nixon, expenditures had doubled to $269 billion. Even when the Vietnam War was over, during the next two fiscal years 1974–76, federal spending had increased again by 35 percent to $366 billion. Another large increase was to occur in fiscal year 1977 with President Ford proposing a budget of $396 billion and the concurrent resolution of Congress calling for an outlay of $413 billion.

In part, this dizzying acceleration of spending was due to the recession itself, which had triggered the "automatic stabilizers" such as unemployment compensation benefits. But most of the spiraling spending was simply a function of the permanent social redistribution programs that were already in place and which had become "uncontrollable."

Why were they "uncontrollable"? One reason was that many of the social programs are endowed with an "entitlement authority" which makes the actual outlay open-ended, depending on the eligibility, rules, and benefit levels established. Various income maintenance programs have been liberalized so that they rise automatically as inflation occurs. Yet other outlays are required by specific laws and contractual agreements. Today approximately three fourths of the federal budget is considered "uncontrollable" because of such incessantly expanding obligations.

In theory, no such thing as an "uncontrollable" budget commitment exists, since Congress controls the nation's purse strings and has the power to determine what the nation shall spend each year. But in political reality men running for Congressional reelection do not choose to eliminate or reduce existing programs. Typically, they keep making promises in exchange for votes and keep piling new programs on top of old ones. What is actually "uncontrollable" are the promises of politicians, who perceive votes as absolute and the budget as infinitely flexible. These "uncontrollable" political promises and government programs must be financed, and they are heavily financed by borrowing from the citizens themselves. Since 1929, deficits have become a cardinal feature of our economic life. There have been deficits in 39 of the last 47 years, and since 1959 those deficits have become huge and virtually permanent. During the single decade 1968–77 the cumulative federal deficits totaled more than $265 billion.

Such federal deficits distorted allocation of resources, damaged the stability of financial markets and, because the money was borrowed from the capital market, inhibited the formation of capital. Since capital investment is necessary for productive growth and high levels of employment, the "uncontrollable" deficits constituted a direct assault on the productive system and a direct cause of unemployment.

In addition to the recorded debt, there developed massive forms of debt which went unrecorded in the official budget numbers: price support programs and a variety of public assistance and social welfare programs to all classes of society. These and many other governmental obligations showed up in the budget, if at all, as footnotes; they were casually described as off-budget items, and the citizens were not aware of them.

We have continued to proliferate both the recorded and unavowed debt at rates substantially greater than the growth of our ability to pay. The visible or acknowledged debt alone has grown at an annual rate of 14 percent in the past decade, while the GNP has grown at a far lower rate. Clearly this system cannot go on indefinitely.

MONETARY POLICY.

Meanwhile, in the Federal Reserve System our monetary policies were being rendered unstable by our fiscal policies.

Indeed, "monetarists" like Milton Friedman would argue that our monetary policies themselves had permitted politicians to get away with irresponsible fiscal policies. Whichever causal relationship you choose, it is certain that the government was printing money hand over fist to help finance its expenditures. The rate of growth in the money supply had risen dangerously. From 1956 to 1965 the money supply expanded at an average annual rate of 2.3 percent. But between 1966 and 1975, as the government engaged in runaway spending and was piling up increasingly huge deficits, the average annual money growth rate rose to 5.8 percent. And in 1976 the announced target for expansion of the money supply was within a range extending from four and a half percent to seven percent. The excessive growth of the money supply further aggravated inflation as more and more dollars chased virtually the same supply of goods and services.

The banking system, encouraged by government policies, was caught up in the go-go craze, both at home and abroad. The once hardhearted banker, who traditionally had demanded too much collateral, suddenly became "our friend," grinning at us from the TV set, encouraging us all to drop in at lunchtime for a quick low-interest loan.

The resultant figures on individual debt tell the tale. In 1945 nonfarm families owed $5.7 billion, consisting primarily of installment debt. By 1974 those debts had risen to $190.1 billion—a leap of 3235 percent.

REGULATION.

Simultaneously government regulation of industry was proliferating, and its effects, too, were simultaneously inflationary and restrictive of productivity. Hundreds of government policies were launched which inhibited the efficiency and effectiveness of our economic system. The result was a mass of regulatory and administrative restrictions on industrial and agricultural production—and a prop to inefficient industries. Where dynamic new industries might have emerged in a free competitive market, regulation was actually maintaining archaic and noncompetitive production systems.

WAGE AND PRICE CONTROLS.

Yet another inflationary explosion was caused by the government's attempt in 1971 and 1972 to pen up the inflation that its own policies had caused. Under the Nixon administration there were three years of wage and price controls. Controls are politically cosmetic and allow the government to be perceived as fighting inflation. In fact, they distorted the economy by rendering impossible the flexible price and wage adjustments needed to allocate resources, and they disrupted competitive relations, diverted capital investment, created shortages, and generated artificial motives for exports. As the record of World War II, the Korean War, and this last peacetime plunge into price controls reveals, federal intervention only suppresses but cannot stop the underlying wage and price pressures. The moment the controls are eliminated, the accumulated distortions that have been building up during the control period burst forth—and a surge of further inflation follows.

These four government policies brought inflation upon us in inexorable fashion. As the administration's chief economic spokesman I was the most visible and vocal fighter against inflation and its major cause, deficit spending. I was fighting, in fact, for a certain constituency that went virtually unrepresented in our allegedly representative government—those millions of Americans who may not have understood the complexities of our economic problems but who knew full well that their taxes were oppressive, that the government was growing steadily more authoritarian, and that their voice was virtually unheard in Washington. I had actually been fighting for that constituency from the moment I took my oath of office under President Nixon as Secretary of the Treasury, and I spoke on behalf of the American taxpayer in every possible forum—from the town halls of the nation to the White House itself.

In 1974 I urged President Nixon to start a systematic campaign against the pathologically inflated budget. I urged him to cut taxes by $20 billion, to be accompanied by a $20 billion reduction in federal spending. But the decision was never made. The tide of Watergate grew ever stronger, and consideration was given to only one concern: beating back impeachment.

After President Nixon resigned, I continued to speak out strongly in the Oval Office. The Congressional elections were nearing, and as the campaign heated up, many Republican politicians were urging President Ford to battle the recession in the typical liberal manner: to loosen up the money supply and cut taxes while boosting federal spending to create make-work jobs for a token number of unemployed. It was, of course, a certain formula for greater inflation and, ultimately, for even greater unemployment.

As debate raged within the administration, I implored President Ford not to follow this destructive formula. "Don't try to cure the economy with the very methods that have wrecked it," I told him. "If we can't finally control inflation, we won't have an economy left to argue about." To his everlasting credit, the President accepted the advice of his counselors and rejected election-eve political compromises. But no sudden cures were possible for an economic crisis which had been building for decades.

I did not confine my battles to government circles. I was equally intent on awakening the public to the dangers of continuing the economically suicidal policies of the past. I accepted every interview I could—from the Asbury Park *Press* to the "Today" show. I logged tens of thousands of miles speaking from Miami to Portland, spelling out the danger. "It took us a hundred and seventy-one years to get a federal budget of a hundred billion dollars a year," I said time and again. "That was 1960. Within nine years we had reached $200 billion and four years later gone over $300 billion. And two years from now, if present trends are not reversed, we will reach $400 billion. *The very existence of our free economy depends on getting government spending under control.*"

It was gratifying that I had succeeded in some measure in taking my case to the people and that President Ford was able to rely on an aroused public to veto 45 spending bills, sustaining 38 of them. This was, I should add, President Ford's most significant political achievement. Even so, the budget deficit soared to $66 billion, the highest in peacetime history.

That, in brief, completes my explanation of the *visible* dimensions of the national economic crisis and of the role I played in combating it.

And now I come to the *invisible* dimensions of that crisis—the philosophical or ideological dimension. I said earlier that one of the most horrifying discoveries I made as I studied the various symptoms and trends in our economy was the presence of a set of quasi-socialist attitudes that have been integrated into the American economy, representing that quest for "a middle ground between communism and capitalism." And it is important to know the genesis of these attitudes. First emerging from the British Fabians in the 1880s, then imported by our own Socialist Party in the 1920s, they were popularly enshrined in the philosophy and approach of Franklin Delano Roosevelt. They constitute, to this day, the core of the liberal "ideology," which is actually committed to a steady erosion of our wealth and freedom, although its advocates are usually unaware of it.

They are unaware of it because they no longer know the relationship between wealth and freedom. Indeed, it is not too much to say that they no longer understand the concept of freedom. FDR actually redefined that concept, corrupting it so hopelessly that, save for a few philosophical diehards, succeeding generations were never again clear as to what it meant. Political freedom means only one thing: freedom *from* the state. FDR, however, invented a new kind of "freedom": a government guarantee of economic security and prosperity. He thus equated "freedom" with cash. By equating the two, FDR corrupted the philosophical concept of freedom. In fact, by calling cash a "freedom" in a society where the state was pledged to protect freedom, he converted "freedom" into a monetary claim on the state. By this single ideological switch, FDR caused a flat reversal of the relationship between the individual and the state in America. The state ceased to be viewed as man's most dangerous enemy, to be shackled forever by constitutional chains. It was henceforth proclaimed to be the precise *opposite*; it became man's tenderhearted protector and provider. Statism and collectivism were brought into this country by the back door—and, ironically, were heralded thereafter as the saving of free enterprise.

To understand the present economic crisis in our country, then, is not just a matter of tracking the problem down to specific "government policies," accurate as such an analysis may be. It requires that we confront the invisible philosophy of government underlying these policies. And of all the rationalizations for authoritarian rule which now surround our form of government, the most essential is this: the belief that the state, under an FDR-like leader, has both the moral obligation and the competence to "run" the economy and guarantee its citizens economic security.

In fact, no one can "run" an economic system. Simply to translate our economy into mathematical terms would, as Oscar Lange demonstrated in 1936, require billions and possibly trillions of equations. It cannot be done. But from FDR on, American Presidents have indeed "run" the economy. And since 1947 their performances have been faithfully recorded in the President's yearly Economic Report to Congress, in accordance with the Employment Act of 1946. Since that law requires that the state guarantee the American people "freedom from want," the President must rise once each year before Congress and solemnly proclaim that either (1) he is *about* to create prosperity and security for all or (2) he has *already* created prosperity and security for all. Those are the only two allowed alternatives. And that means essentially that America's Presidents have been legally mandated to engage in intellectual fraud. The citizen who wants to confront the history of this fraud need merely go to the library, ask for the President's yearly reports to Congress and read them.

From 1947 to 1975 these statements were a sad collection of fiscal irresponsibility and intellectual fraud. Then, in 1975, Gerald Ford made his first statement to Congress. And for the first time in the history of the Presidential literature composed for the Employment Act of 1946, the report represented stark, unadorned truth. Mr. Ford's first sentence was: "The economy is in a severe recession. Unemployment is too high and will rise higher." There was nothing else the man could say. *The U.S. economy was finally in crisis. The illusion that a President, guided by a small number of intellectuals, could "run" our economy had exploded in our faces.*

All this, then, is the invisible dimension of our economic crisis. In financial terms it is desperately grave, but it is the symptom of something graver by far: an unstated philosophical commitment by our governing institutions to the "heresy" of the '30s, the belief that, as Walter Lippmann put it, "there are no limits to man's capacity to govern others." So long as we remain in the grip of that "heresy," we must continue stumbling blindly in the direction of economic catastrophe.

I genuinely do not know whether we will or will not

ultimately survive the desperate damage our government has done to our economy. The potential power of the economy is immense, and its regenerative power *in freedom* is incalculably great. I am prepared to say, however, that a financial collapse is not only possible but probable unless we reverse almost a half century of irrational and unrealistic policies. And I am also certain that should such a collapse occur, we will simultaneously turn to economic dictatorship. Many, perhaps most, of our citizens have been trained by now to see the state as economically omniscient and omnipotent and to blame all economic evils on "business." Should a great economic disaster come, such people will demand a takeover of the major means of production by the state. Given our immense number of legal precedents for intervention and an ideology which morally justifies it, it would not take much to accomplish such a transition. It would be legal. And just as in Britain, it would occur simultaneously with a thunderous proclamation from the left that we were still a "free" society.

V

New York:
Disaster in Microcosm

> The key determinant of the city's budget is the
> politics of the municipal labor unions. Yet the
> public does not elect these leaders. On the
> contrary, it is they, in partnership with the
> political system, who do the electing. The single
> most crucial reason for the death of New York is
> the fact that most critical decisions about the
> future of the city are made to preserve this alliance.
> —JOEL HARNETT, *Chairman,*
> *City Club of New York*

In 1975 New York City collapsed financially. The catastrophe
was not a result of the recession. Nor was it a result of the energy
crisis. It was a problem unique to New York—but unique in only
one sense. The philosophy that has ruled our nation for 40 years
had emerged in large measure from that very city which was
America's intellectual headquarters, and inevitably, it was
carried to its fullest expression in that city. *In the collapse of
New York those who chose to understand it could see a
terrifying dress rehearsal of the fate that lies ahead for this
country if it continues to be guided by the same philosophy of
government.*

As a specialist in municipal bonds I had known for years that
New York was borrowing heavily to finance the promises of its
politicians to the New York electorate. In New York people won
elections exclusively by using the word "more": more public
services of all kinds for the working and middle classes; ever
greater salaries and pensions for the hundreds of thousands who
worked for the New York City government; more extensive
social programs for the less fortunate. All these had been

considered political absolutes, and notes and bonds were sold to finance them. By the end of 1974 the city was seeking to sell about $600 million of bonds every month to finance delivery on the campaign promises. Until 1974 the system worked. But in that year the borrowing pace stepped up ominously. New York's need for funds suddenly seemed to be insatiable.

Then, in February 1975, after a young lawyer representing Bankers Trust discovered, apparently by accident, that the city did not have the tax receipts required by law to secure a $260 million note sale, both Bankers Trust and Chase Manhattan refused to go through with the underwriting. Fully aware that New York might not be able to honor its debts, investors by the tens of thousands refused to buy any more New York paper.

The market had spoken. Investors had recognized that purchase of the notes would make them just another vulnerable layer in the borrowing pyramid and that they could be repaid only by the creation of still more layers of debt in the months ahead. They simply shied away, choosing instead from a variety of competing investment opportunities. The shock of New York's financial collapse was explosive—in New York, in the rest of the country, and throughout the world. How could it have happened so suddenly? In fact, it had not happened suddenly. What was "sudden" was the traumatic discovery by the financial community that it was being rooked in a Ponzi game.

There was only one response from New York's officials when they lost their "credibility," as the quaint expression goes. Faced with the closing of the market, they howled with self-pity and demanded federal aid in the form of a Treasury guarantee of their loans. I explained that we did not possess that authority; indeed, I could not support the idea even if we did. I made this essential point: If the federal government were to step in to guarantee New York City's bonds, we would be asking other taxpayers across the land to subsidize New York's deficit spending, and the government would inevitably be forced to supply similar protection to other cities. That, I said, would make a mockery of the principles of federalism on which the nation was founded. And, I concluded, if the federal government did assist New York City, it could be only under the most stringent of conditions. After I explained my position at a Senate hearing on October 1, the New York *Post* rolled off the presses with the screaming headline SIMON ON U.S. AID:

MAKE CITY SUFFER. And when President Ford attacked the "disease" of runaway spending and criticized New York City for "asking the rest of the country to guarantee its bills," his position was summed up by the New York *Daily News* with the headline FORD TO CITY: DROP DEAD.

What the "defenders" of New York found most difficult to endure was the fact that the American public was responding to the principles enunciated by the Administration, not to their demands. Mail to Congress strongly opposed a federal bailout. California Senator Alan Cranston reported that his letters ran 95 percent against a bailout. And a Charleston, S.C., newspaper poll produced 7604 votes to 263 against Mayor Beame and Company. *Newsweek*, reporting on this popular reaction, interpreted it as an expression of popular antipathy toward New York but conceded that Ford had touched "a real and rising concern about profligacy in government at every level."

What were the facts? Where had New York's money gone?

The Treasury Department made an extensive analysis of New York's spending pattern based on a comparison between New York and other major American cities in 1973. The study showed that New York had gone out of fiscal control in a significant way that was not to be found in any other city. New York was spending in excess of three times more per capita than any city with a population of more than one million. When the base was broadened to include smaller cities, only Boston and Baltimore were remotely comparable, and even when compared to these cities, New York's expenses were 50 percent higher.

Clearly, the most significant factor in New York's financial collapse was the cost of maintaining its municipal work force. New York employed some 49 employees per 1000 residents. The payrolls of virtually all other major cities ranged from 30 to 32 employees per 1000 inhabitants. More striking yet were the salaries paid to New York public employees, which were among the highest in the country and far outstripped comparable salaries in the private sector. A subway changemaker, who was not required to change anything higher than a $10 bill, earned $212 per week, a teller in a commercial bank earned $150 per week. A city porter earned $203; in private industry an X-ray technician earned $187. Teachers in the secondary school system earned up to $23,750, considerably more than counterparts in the private schools, and their workload had declined.

If public salaries were absurd, the pensions of the city's

workers were appalling. Between 1960 and 1970, 54 pension bills
had been passed in New York. In 1961 the city paid $260.8
million to provide its employees with retirement and Social
Security benefits. By 1972 that sum had jumped 175 percent, to
$753.9 million, the growth in city employment accounting for
only 30 percent of the increase. And by 1975 the city budget for
retirement benefits had grown to $1.3 billion. Calculations
showed that by 1985 pensions would cost New York City $3
billion a year.

These dollar totals do not tell the full story, for there are
other hidden costs that accompany these extraordinary pension
payments. For example, police and transit workers can retire
after 20 years at half their final pay. Thus, trained men in their
late 30s and early 40s are able to quit and take other jobs while
they collect city pensions.

Under these circumstances, it is actually bizarre that the
liberal position on the New York crisis rests on the charge that
New York has gone broke because of its *welfare* burden, because
of its "decency to the poor."

Actually, New York's subsidies to the middle classes have
been overwhelmingly greater than its subsidies to the poor.
Writing in *Commentary* in May 1976, James Ring Adams noted
that the city's official explanation for its fiscal embarrassment
"was not only misleading, it is almost the exact opposite of the
truth." He continued: "The most important source of its
problem...is *not* the city's generosity to the poor and
downtrodden, but its attempt to subsidize large portions of the
middle class, including its own employees."

Adams pointed out that most of the city's tax revenues go to
employees' salaries, pensions, and fringe benefits—all directed
to the middle class. Worse yet, the middle class absorbs a
significant percentage of the funds allegedly allotted to the poor.
Adams reported, for example, that day-care programs, financed
by Medicaid benefits, were serving a large number of middle-
class families. According to a mayoral task force report, more
than one third of the children attending day-care centers were
found to be ineligible. Similarly, a recent study by Dr. Trude
Lash found that some 100,000 middle-class children were
receiving welfare. And ultimately, much of the budgets for New
York's welfare projects end up in the pockets of their
administrators, who are members of the middle class.

It is blatantly obvious that the subsidy to New York's middle

class—above all, the salaries, pensions and fringe benefits paid
to the government workers—is responsible for New York's fiscal
collapse. The officials of New York's budget commission
concluded in 1975 that a pay freeze for all city employees could
save between $400 and $600 million of Mayor Beame's $641.5
million budget gap. If New York's public employees had not
been remunerated in so lavish a fashion, had they been paid by
the standard of other big cities, the city would not have been in
debt at all. Instead, the city would have had a *surplus* of between
$500 million and $1 billion.

Not only had New York been subsidizing a significant
portion of its middle class, but the victims—the *unsubsidized*
portion of the population—had begun to disappear. Quite
simply, those who were being forced to pay these extortionate
subsidies to their fellow citizens were running away.

For more than a decade New York City has been slowly
losing its productive backbone. Industry and skilled workers, hit
by New York's excessive tax rate, have been leaking out of the
city at a rapid rate. Between December 1974 and December 1975
alone, according to the Bureau of Labor Statistics, 143,000 jobs
disappeared.

One sees plainly that nothing has destroyed New York's
finances but the liberal political formula. Using the "poor" as a
compulsive pretext, New York politicians have formed a
working coalition with a portion of the middle class to run the
city for their mutual benefit at the expense of the rest of the
productive population. And inevitably that productive population has slowly withdrawn, gradually destroying the city's
economic base. Liberal politics, endlessly glorifying its own
"humanism," has, in fact, been annihilating the very conditions
for human survival.

An analyst with insight into the liberal genesis of the disaster
was Theodore White. Writing in *New York* on November 10,
1975, he said:

"There are over a million people on welfare in this city.
Our 260,000 city employees have wives, or husbands, and
children. Most of them vote—and they are all united in
one great purpose: "More." No one can be elected in this
city who promises "Less." So all our politicians for 20
years have promised more—more police, more schools,
more playgrounds, more guidance counselors, bigger

pensions, more hospital beds, more admissions to our university system. *Together the welfare population and the city employees dominate our electoral politics.* As in a giant soviet, they elect their bosses and paymaster...."

As Secretary of the Treasury I described the cheating employed by these bosses in the most moderate language possible: "In recent years, New York has faced the marketplace's demands for restraint, responsibility, and realism with spending, promises, and *gimmickry.* Capital borrowing for current expenditures, *artificially high revenue estimates to 'balance' budgets and support even more borrowing,* and, above all, an inability to say no where more spending is concerned make New York unique among our major cities."

Others who were not serving as the financial spokesman for the administration allowed themselves more explicit language. Again, in *New York* magazine on June 2, 1975, Chris Welles described the two principal manifestations of the city's dishonesty:

> Accounting trickery evolved into a refined art at City Hall. The techniques were abstruse and varied. But basically, most involved time warps—specifically, pretending that expenses the city was incurring now actually wouldn't be incurred until later and that revenues the city expected to receive later had already been received. ... The city had also been selling notes in anticipation of income it knew might never arrive at all.

How, finally, was the problem solved? It wasn't. Or, more precisely, there was a political uproar culminating in a cosmetic "solution" as New York fought incessantly to deny, and to escape from the consequences of its financial folly.

As I have already said, my position as Secretary of the Treasury had been reduced by the press to the slogan "Make City Suffer." In fact, from the very beginning of the crisis, we at Treasury had been seeking some technical and constitutional means of assisting the city.

When the market closed to New York in March 1975, we held a series of meetings with experts in municipal finance. We were trying to identify the cause of the market closure and to see if the problem could be resolved in time to permit the city to sell $550 million of notes on April 15. Simultaneously we were seeking at Treasury to establish whether the federal government could be of assistance. But for this we needed facts—facts about the city's expenses and obligations, facts about its revenue sources, facts about its debt structure. It was a severe shock to all of us when we found that no such facts were then obtainable. No one in New York City could provide us with a document that set forth the income and expenses of the city, its assets and liabilities.

Still, we persisted in trying to find some form of federal assistance for New York's problem. We were looking for an authentic solution—a treatment for the cause of the problem, not a mask for its symptoms. American taxpayers could not be drained to fill New York's bottomless pit, and whatever solution we devised had to be applicable to other American cities as well.

In the course of many meetings with New York officials, we demanded a commitment to the idea that New York spending had to be brought into line with revenues. We received no such commitment. New York's political leaders were wholly bent on extracting money from the nation's taxpayers and acted as if our demands were absurd. According to Mayor Beame and his colleagues, you could not fight the powerful forces for spending that were destroying the city. We understood quite well, of course, that if these politicians actually moved to cut out the parasitical incrustations which were strangling the city, they would be at war with their own electorate. They would not and did not act to solve the problem. The truth was that there was no way that rational reform could be instituted without some type of default or bankruptcy proceedings so that the unpayable debt could be extended in time. This was well understood by the top financial and legal advisers of Mayor Beame. But Beame and other New York politicians would not tolerate so public a confession of their failure. I learned early that political facesaving was more important to them than the life of the city itself.

Whether the New York politicians would tolerate it or not, however, I had to examine the likelihood of a default of New York and to estimate its impact on the financial institutions of the country. An analysis was made by economists at both the Treasury and the Federal Reserve Board, who indicated that the impact of such a default might be psychologically explosive but that financially it would be highly contained and short-lived. Our analysts uniformly believed that there was enough underlying value in New York City to assure that all bond- and noteholders could eventually be paid 100 cents on the dollar.

Given this conviction that the economic impact of a default by New York would be brief and contained, we reached the conclusion I have already described: that the Treasury should offer no help to New York until and unless a powerful commitment was first made to adopt a responsible fiscal program.

This could scarcely be summarized as a desire to punish New York, to see it suffer or "drop dead." Nonetheless, that is how my position was presented to the public by much of the press. In fact, every recommendation I was to make met with the same distortion, whether it was a suggestion that New York charge tuition at its city colleges; that it scrap rent control to return the dying real estate industry to life and augment the tax base; that it replace city employees in a variety of services—above all, in health and sanitation—with private contractors, who would perform the same work at the lower prices; that it briefly boost the sales tax. To all such specific recommendations to cut New York expenses and raise its income, New York politicians and members of the press responded with personal invective: I was either "inhumane" or "Simple Simon." The suggestions themselves were never considered.

At the same time, city officials, union leaders and even members of the financial community raised the specter of a nationwide financial collapse. Felix Rohatyn, general partner of Lazard Freres, chairman of Municipal Assistance Corporation (MAC), and unofficial spokesman for New York's financial community, testified to the Senate: "I have given it as my professional judgment that the impact of a city default would inevitably lead to a default of major state agencies and a possible default of New York State itself...A default of mammoth proportions involving city and state...would be an inexcusable tragedy." It was obvious to many members of Congress that this was blackmail. During the hearings in October 1975 of the Senate Banking Committee, Utah Senator Jake Garn said: "I do think we are seeing a propaganda battle that overstates the effect on the rest of this nation...whoever is doing it, is doing a fantastic job of convincing the whole country that we are going to go down the river if New York defaults on its bonds. I think it is being greatly overplayed to put pressure on the Congress to come up with some kind of bailout program."

If the threat of a national collapse was not sufficiently frightening, many of the same people spawned an even more horrifying domino theory. If New York defaulted, they said, all financial systems in the entire world would collapse! Rohatyn announced somberly that a New York default would be perceived internationally as evidence of "the failure of capitalism." And David Rockefeller, whose bank held the most New York paper, rushed about frantically warning financial leaders all over the world that the entire international financial system would disintegrate if New York defaulted.

The horrifying scenario of international financial collapse did not materialize, of course. The world market was aware that New York could not pay its debts, and it did not fall to pieces. The New York crisis was the potential disaster in microcosm; it was not the disaster itself.

For the most part, Congress was not eager to bail out New York. The responsible men were as aware as I of the constitutional pitfalls of such a bailout, and the less responsible discovered that their constituencies would not tolerate it. They were willing, as I was, to assist New York if a mode of assistance could be discovered which would not set a destructive precedent for other cities and if New York City showed authentic signs of self-correction. Within this shared context, however, the liberal leadership differentiated itself by a ritual keening over New York's crucifixion on behalf of the "poor" and by ritual denunciation of those of us in the administration who named the problem in other, more realistic terms.

Nonetheless, liberal Congressmen were no more willing than conservative Congressmen to put a federal guarantee behind the spending patterns of New York City which, even by the most softheaded standards, were inexcusable. But the pressure from all sides was enormous. The fear campaign and blackmail from all groups had their effect, and in a political forum, the result was inevitable: A compromise was sought. I discussed the situation at great length with President Ford, and we agreed we could not yield on principle. We could not support any federal guarantee of New York's bonds, and we could not tolerate the foisting of New York's debt on the rest of the nation. The only possible compromise we could accede to was a short-term loan, with the most stringent conditions of repayment.

Thus, in December 1975, Congress enacted and President Ford signed into law, legislation authorizing me to make loans of up to $2.3 billion a year through mid-1978 to enable New York to meet its seasonal cash needs. In addition, Congress mandated a one percent override so that the Treasury would actually profit from the arrangement.

On Christmas Day, Assistant Secretary Bob Gerard met with me and Treasury Counsel Dick Albrecht to draw up the agreement. The loan was protected by an airtight guarantee: The revenues of New York City and New York State were earmarked first and foremost for repayment. There was not the slightest danger that the Treasury would lose one cent. In return for the loan, the city and state were required to make decisions of a type they had heretofore refused to make. In addition to committing themselves to a program of cuts with the goal of balancing the budget by 1978, they were forced to admit finally that they could not repay a substantial number of their noteholders—and to announce a three-year moratorium.

Most of the press, however, failed entirely to understand that New York had indeed defaulted. *Time* magazine, under the headline LAST-MINUTE BAILOUT OF A CITY ON THE BRINK, wrote:

> To wangle the loan, *which was necessary to prevent default*, city and state officials were forced to take drastic actions that went against many a past promise. For the most highly taxed city in the country, the state legislature passed a $200 million increase that includes a 25 percent raise in the city income tax. . . . *Also approved was a three-year moratorium on the redemption of $1.6 billion in city short-term debts held by individuals.* [My italics.]

Time did not grasp that in reality a default *was* a "moratorium" on payments. And *Time* was not alone. The short-term loan granted by the Treasury under these conditions was hailed by politicians and press as a victory for "New York" and a capitulation by the Treasury. Many in the press exulted over my alleged "cave-in." They got the notion, not from the facts but from the facesaving formulations of the New York politicians. Governor Carey pronounced the loan a "vindication of New York's cause."

With rare exceptions—the outstanding one being *New York* magazine—the press had simply covered the crisis as though it had been a boxing match between good guys ("New York") and bad guys (Ford, Burns, and Simon). I was constantly shocked by the lack of seriousness, by the lack of concern for fact, and, where I was personally concerned, by many journalists' failure to understand that I was not simply a malignant symbol to be hissed at in ritual hate, but a representative of a serious economic and constitutional position.

I found some comfort in a piece in *Columbia Journalism Review* written by Martin Mayer, author of *The Bankers*.

Mayer was one of the few writers in America who understood the situation. He, too, had testified before the Senate Banking Committee, but unlike most other witnesses, he spoke in clear, unevasive English. He identified the union contracts and pensions as the critical source of New York's collapse, he analyzed the frauds and fiscal sleight-of-hand by city and state, he called for a formal declaration of bankruptcy, and although he believed that some federal aid would prove necessary, he implored Congress not to give New York assistance in any form which would allow the New York political establishment to go on pretending that it could muddle through. His testimony had been strikingly candid:

> ... When a man tells you he can take $1.8 billion out of debt service and he is still $1 billion short, but you should give him a guarantee, I don't see how you can listen to him.
>
> Nothing, nothing can work that pretends that a history of incompetence and fraud is really a history of social concern and bad luck, or that an insolvency problem is really a cash flow problem.

But the clarity of Mayer's understanding was rare, and it certainly was not shared by most of those who wrote about New York. Indeed, the press failed in its chief function: to serve the people as watchdogs of government. Most of the watchdogs of New York City were totally bewildered by the fraud, misappropriation of funds, deception of investors, and ultimate bankruptcy—all "necessitated" by liberal ideals.

An almost oceanic self-pity was to dominate the electoral period of 1976. During that period it was morally mandatory for all liberal Democrats running for office to portray New York as a city crucified for its compassion to the poor and to demand the federalization of welfare. The Senatorial campaign in New York City revealed the magnitude of this delusional interpretation of the New York crisis. Democrat Daniel Patrick Moynihan, who knew better, felt compelled to join the liberal chorus. He won the election. Conservative Republican Senator James Buckley, the only major politician in New York who had been immaculately honest with his constituency, was classified as "hostile to New York." He lost the election. The truth was still intolerable.

On the Presidential level candidate Jimmy Carter, too, was sucked into the New York hysteria. While campaigning initially as a conservative, he had taken a hard fiscal line on New York, and he had told the *New York Times* that "it would be inappropriate to single out New York City for special favors." He had also stated his opposition to the federalization of welfare. To get the backing of New York politicians, however, he shifted and won Abe Beame's endorsement in exchange for a fuzzy promise to concern himself with New York. By the time Carter arrived at the Democratic convention, he and the Democratic Party were strongly advocating a federal takeover of welfare.

But a Democratic administration did not solve New York's problem. The election over, neither Mr. Moynihan in the Senate nor Jimmy Carter in the White House could permit themselves the act of subsidizing New York's intransigent irresponsibility. And reality kept exacting its toll of the city. On March 9, 1977, with a collapse a few days away, the city was faced by newly intransigent banks and a Carter Treasury which was refusing a bailout on precisely the same grounds as its predecessor. The only distinction, in fact, between the Carter and Ford administrations was that Carter kept exuding affable sounds and vague promises. Then Mayor Beame once again pulled a fiscal maneuver out of a hat. The city, he declared, could pay a $1 billion debt by selling Mitchell-Lama mortgages, by the city unions' agreement to forgo payment on MAC bonds they already held, and by cash from various sources. Steven R. Weisman, a New York *Times* reporter, put it accurately:

> ...So confusing and complicated was the package produced...that Mr. Beame and [City Comptroller Harrison J.] Goldin could not agree how to describe it.

It was the same old New York routine, but this time the bulk of the anticipated funds would come from the subsidized middle classes. New York now had no recourse except to feed systematically off its own gifts to its politically favored groups. On the basis of this alleged "solution" to the New York problem, the Carter administration approved the short-term loan to New York. It was essentially the same "solution" that had taken place under the Ford administration. Some change had occurred, of course. The banks had learned something. They were now refusing to lend money at all without hard external rule over New York politicians and criminal sanctions for disobedience— a demand that Beame, as usual, considered "humiliating."

The New York press had also learned something. It now customarily considered the "honesty" of New York's fiscal decisions. And outside the city Americans had profited by the horrifying object lesson. States across the country were scrutinizing the budget practices of their own cities. And a few liberal governors, in particular Jerry Brown of California and Ella Grasso of Connecticut, were taking hard looks at state employment rolls and costly welfare programs. Particularly during the electoral period, "fiscal responsibility" was a buzzword in all political discourse.

Yet, on the most fundamental philosophical level, little had changed. Very few liberals had yet learned that a government job was not an alternative mode of producing wealth. Liberals were still singing hosannahs to government jobs as "solutions" to unemployment and to ostentatious government programs to rescue the "poor." They still perceived business as an infinitely taxable resource. They still fundamentally believed that the real source of money was the Treasury printing press. Above all, nothing had dented the official liberal position that the whole gigantic mess in New York had been motivated by "compassion."

The painful truth is that 40 years of liberal "compassion" has created a politics of stealing from productive Peter to pay nonproductive Paul, creating a new class of Americans which lives off our taxes and pretends that its institutionalized middle-class pork barrel is all for the sake of the "poor." But no one in office today dares challenge either the formula or its rationalization, assuming he even understands it. There actually is no *political* solution in a situation where the truth has become politically lethal.

If New York were a discrete political entity, disconnected from America and committing suicide in a unique way, it would be sad but not frightening. But it is frightening, for New York is not disconnected from America. It is America's premier city and its intellectual headquarters. It is America in microcosm—the philosophy, the illusions, the pretensions, and the rationalizations which guide New York City are those which guide the entire country. What is happening to New York, therefore, is overwhelmingly important to all Americans, and it is imperative that they understand it. If they do not repudiate the ideas that justify this system of government, then New York's present must inevitably become America's future.

VI

U.S.A.: The Macrocosm

> I have no respect for the passion for equality,
> which seems to me merely idealizing envy.
> —OLIVER WENDELL HOLMES, JR.

Most Americans believe that "dictatorship" means the arrival on the political scene of a little man with a mustache, wearing a khaki suit, shouting Marxist slogans or "Sieg Heil" and slaughtering ethnic minorities in the name of the "proletariat" or the "race." This is extremely convenient for those clean-shaven gentlemen in business suits who haven't the faintest intention of slaughtering ethnic minorities and who are seeking dictatorial powers over the American people in the name of the "public interest." It has enabled them to lay the groundwork for an economic dictatorship which is expanding geometrically year after year.

The essence of dictatorship, if one understands that concept in principle, means that the state is using its police powers not to protect individual liberty, but to violate it. And there has been almost total silence about the entrenched bureaucratic dictatorship that is directly affecting millions and indirectly damaging the lives and well-being of literally everyone in the country.

The direct victims are the producers of America. Ranging from the littlest farmer or proprietor of a mom-and-pop store to the great industrial giants, they are living under an unceasing barrage of violations of their liberty, of edicts that prevent them from engaging in the simplest and most reasonable activities, of absurd, unintelligible, and self-contradictory acts of coercion. The best way to get a sense of the breadth and detail of this problem is by giving you some case histories.

60

Truckers traveling along the main cross-country interstate routes between Cleveland, Ohio, and Jacksonville, Florida, must ride with their trailers empty even though shippers at both ends of the line are eager to give them profitable cargo. Why? Because the Interstate Commerce Commission permits the truckers to haul freight only one way.

A bus company with an excellent safety record— Greyhound—was hauled into federal court by the Labor Department, claiming that the age qualifications for the drivers of its giant buses were discriminatory and that the company should hire people to drive no matter how old. The company was next assaulted by the Equal Employment Opportunity Commission (EEOC) on its height requirement for drivers—its safety people having set the minimum height at five feet seven inches—and along with this came a government demand that Greyhound pay about $19 million in back pay to unspecified, unknown short individuals.

A responsible meat-packing plant—Armour—was ordered by the Federal Meat Inspection Service to create an aperture in a sausage conveyor line so that inspectors could take out samples to test. The company created the aperture. Along came another federal agency, the Occupational Safety and Health Administration (OSHA), and demanded that the aperture be closed as a safety hazard. Each federal agency threatened to shut down the plant if it did not comply instantly with its order.

The Southern Railway Company developed a new vehicle— the Big John Car—to haul grain at rates up to one-third cheaper than conventional boxcars. The Interstate Commerce Commission banned the innovation and refused Southern permission to slash rates on the grounds that it would be unfair to other railroads and to truckers. Only after spending four years and millions of dollars in legal costs was Southern finally given the go-ahead to cut costs.

Three thousand companies have canceled pension plans for their employees after receiving the complex regulations of the Employee Retirement Income Security Act (ERISA). The requirements were so costly that the only alternative was to scrap the pension plans. Before ERISA's rulings were handed down, 5000 companies a month were requesting IRS approval of pension plans. After ERISA's edicts, the number decreased to fewer than 2000 a month.

These case histories give you some sense of what is happening to the productive institutions of America. And even these examples do not really communicate what is happening because there is no way for the human mind to encompass the full reality. No one alive even knows how many federal regulations over business there are. To list all the rulings and regulations established in 1976 alone—just one year—required 57,027 pages of fine print in the *Federal Register*. Interstate Commerce Commission rulings—applicable only to the regulation of interstate transportation—number in the *trillions*. The evidence clearly indicates that the regulatory process has run amok, reaching far beyond legitimate concern over such values as health, safety, and protection of the environment. This is a *disease* of government; it is not government.

The costs to American industry of this incredible torrent of governmental edicts and rulings are so immense and of so many kinds that they defy the imagination. Yet apart from the financial losses of billions of dollars, the sheer paperwork forced on these companies by Congress and the executive is draining a fortune out of the economy. According to the Commission on Federal Paperwork, government agencies print about ten billion sheets of paper a year to be completed by U.S. businesses. Each year the government spends at least $15 billion to process paperwork.

That is scandalous enough. But the economic impact on small business is frightful. Collectively America's small businessmen are forced to spend from $15 to $20 billion simply in completing government paperwork. A typical small business with a gross income of less than $30,000 is required to file 53 forms.

The figures become astronomical when the companies are large. General Motors must detail 22,300 employees to federal paperwork; the "affirmative action" files alone make a stack about twice as high as their New York headquarters.

When Eli Lilly & Company asked the Food and Drug Administration recently to approve a new drug for arthritis, the application ran to 120,000 pages, many in duplicate and triplicate, and two small trucks were required to transport the load to Washington. Indeed, Lilly officials are forced to spend more man-hours on federal paperwork than to research new drugs for cancer and heart disease. Clearly this is economic insanity.

As billions in capital and manpower are allocated to the task of obeying bureaucratic orders, there is an inevitable decline in productivity and in technological innovation. The regulatory agencies are functioning as a "stop growth" force. Allegedly protectors of life, they are heralds of slow death.

It is obvious that no such viciously arbitrary assault on the American productive system could occur were it not backed up by the police powers of the state. And in form, as well as in substance, the regulatory bureaucracy is dictatorial. The rulings of American regulatory agencies are largely unintelligible, and accordingly the American businessman is cowed into submission and a state of permanent fear. He has no way today of knowing what the law is or whether he is in compliance with it. Not only are many of these regulations self-contradictory and mutually contradictory, but they are also written by government lawyers in a horrendous bureaucratic jargon which increases their impenetrability. The agencies themselves cannot understand many of their own rulings.

Chairman Robert D. Moran of the Occupational Safety and Health Review Commission, the independent agency created to hear businessmen's appeals from OSHA rulings, says that "there isn't a person on earth who can be certain he is in full compliance with the requirements of this standard at any particular point in time." Yet businessmen are persistently penalized for their failure to meet such unintelligible standards. This is the unmistakable mark of Big Brother.

Another characteristic of a dictatorial regime is that it is above the law. No checks and balances exist to limit its power. And that, too, characterizes the regulatory bureaucracies. In theory, these agencies are responsible to the executive and/or Congress and subject to review by the courts. In practice, no one has any means of supervising this monstrous collection of regulatory edicts. Unless an occasional regulation arouses a public furor, as in the case of the ban on saccharin in diet drinks, Congress does not inquire into the day-by-day operations of the agencies.

Indeed, the regulatory agencies tend to operate outside the American legal system. Conventionally described as "extrajudiciary," these agencies simultaneously function as investigators, detectives, policemen, prosecutors, judges and juries. And it is commonplace that they hold businessmen guilty until proved innocent. Unless an American business is immensely rich and can afford to fight the long battle to take its case to a higher court, it has little or no protection from the arbitrary decisions of the regulatory bureaucracies.

Finally, I must add to all this the fact that the United States imposes a higher corporate profits tax than any other nation. Indeed, corporate profits are taxed twice—a unique penalty to which no one else in America is subjected and against which I fought vainly before an indifferent Congress. Our corporate taxation policies punish the competent producer, inhibit capital formation and restrict industrial growth. Add to this the notoriously foggy antitrust laws which are constantly used by the regulatory bureaucracy of the Justice Department not merely to safeguard competition but to chop down the most competitively successful companies in the very name of competition!

All this pressure is wrought in the name of the public interest.

Since the '60s the vast bulk of the regulatory legislation passed by Congress and the hundreds of thousands of elaborations in the forms of regulatory rulings have been largely initiated by a powerful new political lobby that goes by the name of the Public Interest movement. This movement represents neither of the conventional economic divisions of the past—i.e., business or labor. It claims, instead, to speak only for the People and concentrates on the wellbeing of "consumers," "environ-ment" and "minorities." These terms, too, are chosen so that one cannot with any comfort challenge them. In fact, the Public Interest movement is a lobby, not for the People, but for expanding police powers of the state over American producers. There have been few more consistently and vehemently anticapitalist groups in the history of America.

What is even more significant about the Public Interest movement, however, is the fact that it is, above all, the political voice of the contemporary urban elite. Irving Kristol analyzed this elite for the first time in the *Wall Street Journal* on May 19, 1975. He called it the "new class":

This "new class".... consists of a goodly proportion of these college-educated people whose skills and vocations proliferate in a "post-industrial society."... We are talking about scientists, teachers and educational admin-istrators, journalists and others in the communications industries, psychologists, social workers, those lawyers and doctors who make their careers in the expanding public sector, city planners, the staffs of the larger foundations, the upper levels of the government bureaucracy, etc., etc....

What does this "new class" want, and why should it be so hostile to the business community? Well, one should understand that the members of this class are "idealistic," in the 1960s sense of that term—i.e., they are not much interested in money but are keenly interested in power. Power for what? The power to shape our civilization—a power which, in a capitalist system, is supposed to reside in the free market....

In sum, says Kristol, the "new class" combines a morbid economic ignorance with a driving power lust, and it combines hostility to democracy with the illusion that it speaks for the People. He warns that if the political ambition of this class is not checked, the dangerous result must be the destruction of freedom: "We shall move toward some version of state capitalism in which the citizen's individual liberty would be rendered ever more insecure."

There are a great many reasons for the development of an economic tyranny in the United States, and historians will eventually assign the blame. But the fault, at least in part, lies with capitalists themselves. Throughout the last century the attachment of businessmen to free enterprise has weakened dramatically as they discovered they could demand—and receive—short-range advantages from the state. To a tragic degree coercive regulation has been invited by businessmen who were unwilling to face honest competition in the free market, with its great risks and penalties as well as its rewards, and by businessmen who have run to the government in search of regulatory favors, protective tariffs and subsidies, as well as those monopolistic powers which only the state can grant.

During my tenure at Treasury, I watched with incredulity as businessmen ran to the government in every crisis, whining for handouts or protection from the very competition that has made this system so productive. I saw Texas ranchers, hit by drought, demanding government-guaranteed loans; giant milk cooperatives lobbying for higher price supports; major airlines fighting deregulation to preserve their monopoly status; huge companies like Lockheed seeking federal assistance to rescue them from sheer inefficiency; bankers like David Rockefeller demanding government bailouts to protect them from their ill-conceived investments; network executives like William Paley of CBS fighting to preserve regulatory restrictions and to block the emergence of competitive cable and pay TV. And always, such gentlemen proclaimed their devotion to free enterprise and their opposition to the arbitrary intervention into our economic life by the state.

My own response to such businessmen was harsh, and I warned those with whom I discussed these practices that they were indeed, as Lenin had predicted, braiding the rope that would be used to hang them. Having said this, however, I still believe it is obvious that business, seen as a whole, is more sinned against than sinning. And this is because of the reigning anti-free enterprise philosophy of our age. Starting in the last century and acquiring its modern style with the New Deal, it has rapidly engulfed a substantial portion of our educated classes. As Kristol shows, egalitarianism is the ruling value system of our urban "elite." And it is no coincidence that egalitarianism and despotism are linked. Historically, they always have been. Hitler and Stalin and Mao all offered their people an egalitarian society, disclosing only when it was too late that some would always be "more equal than others."

The equality peddled by egalitarianism is *not* the equality referred to in the American Constitution, although history is being rapidly rewritten to suggest that it is. Our Founding Fathers and the liberal—i.e., procapitalist—philosophers of that era were in full rebellion against an almost unbroken human history of the divine right of kings and of legal and social tyranny rooted in hereditary privilege. When they declared that "all men are created equal," they meant that men were equal before the law, that no legal chains forged by ancestry or caste should bind any individual to a permanent underclass. They meant that men should share an equal opportunity to face the challenges of life, each free to achieve what he could and rise to the level he could by his own wit, effort and merit. This is the quintessentially American philosophy. Slavery and institution-alized racism clearly violate this principle, but in no sense do they render it less glorious.

The revolutionary effect of such a concept of legal equality created a nation with unprecedented social mobility, as men escaped by millions from the feudal prison of a hereditary class system. And as they escaped, as individuals of different kinds followed their own paths, what emerged was immense diversity and, inevitably, different levels of achievement. Our Constitution annihilated hereditary aristocracy—and replaced it with a competitive *meritocracy*.

The egalitarians' equality is of a profoundly different kind. The system they seek to create is the precise opposite of a meritocracy. The more one achieves, the more one is punished; the less one achieves, the more one is rewarded. Its goal is not to enhance individual achievement; it is to *level* all men.

What we are seeing in America today is government dedicated to both halves of the egalitarian leveling process: the chopping down of those who produce wealth and the transfer of that wealth from those who have earned it to those who have not. I have already briefly described the regulatory agencies' assault on the producers. I will now describe the transfer process. It is, of course, our welfare system.

There are a great many things to be said about our welfare system, and a thousand different books are saying them. I wish, here, to make one principal point: that its primary purpose today is a concern *not* to assist the helpless, but to redistribute the wealth. I am not speculating about people's motives here; I am talking about what is actually happening to the taxes that the government takes from the productive citizens of this land.

To see the pattern clearly, one must stand back and look at the welfare system in the full context of government spending. The context is this—and I use 1976 figures:

—The Gross National Product, meaning the wealth created by our productive citizenry: $1,609.5 billion.
—The federal budget, equivalent to 22.8 percent of the GNP: $366.5 billion.
—The national debt (not including the off-budget items), to be paid by future taxes on the earnings of the productive: $631.9 billion.

What part of this disastrous explosion of expenditure and debt is actually going to the authentically helpless among us?

The group we hear the most about are families with dependent children. It has certainly generated the most protests. We know that Aid to Families with Dependent Children (AFDC) has been a federal invitation to fathers to abandon their families, in reality or in appearance; the system is clearly corrupt. Yet the sum it received in 1976 was only $8.3 billion.

The second group that can be legitimately viewed as meriting assistance is the disabled—the blind, crippled, and handicapped of all ages, including veterans who cannot sustain their own lives or do so with extreme difficulty. The sum paid to this group in 1976 was $25 billion.

If one takes both the dependent children and the disabled together—the two genuinely helpless groups in the nation—the budget for their support totaled $33 billion. The sum is enormous, but it constitutes less than ten percent of the national budget. It has *not* been the payments to the helpless and disabled that have generated our incredible budget.

Is that calamitous budget due perhaps to defense expenditures? That, of course, is what liberals have been screaming in unison for years. Actually, the 1976 defense budget was $101 billion, 24 percent of the budget—*down* from 46.9 percent in 1963. Clearly, it is not the defense budget, with its declining share of the national taxes, that is hurling this nation into bankruptcy.

For what, then, is the remainder of the budget earmarked? A large chunk—$37 billion in 1976—goes for interest on the national debt. But most federal dollars go for "social programs" of one kind or another. And for whom are these programs intended? A very substantial percentage of them—certainly more than half—are benefiting the *middle class*.

This is so shockingly different from what is commonly supposed to be the case that it requires demonstration. It is easy enough to do. All that is needed is a brief inspection of the two relevant categories of federal budgeting: the official welfare programs in the national budget and the off-budget items to be guaranteed or financed in the future.

First, the national budget. Sixty percent of the budget is explicitly earmarked for social welfare. In 1976 these expenditures totaled $198.3 billion (with the states and local governments spending another $133 billion). Where did the federal dollars go?

One chunk—$31.2 billion—went to pensions with built-in cost-of-living escalation for federal Civil Service employees, veterans and retired railroad workers. This sum was only slightly less than the total sum allotted to both AFDC and the disabled. Clearly, this sum was *not* primarily of benefit to the hard-core poor.

Another chunk of the federal welfare budget went to unemployment compensation—$15.4 billion. This payment is allotted to the ablebodied who are temporarily out of work and is intended to sustain them while they actively seek new jobs. The total was unusually large because of the recession, but that by no means accounted for all of it. Like all gigantic outlays of federal funds, this one has become a magnet to free riders. A study made during the worst of the recession in 1975 indicated that about half the people who had lost jobs were not looking for work at all but were living on unemployment compensation. Indeed, for years, collecting unemployment has become a way of life for a significant number of people who hold a job just long enough to qualify for payments—collect for the full period—get another job and hold it long enough to qualify—collect, etc., etc. Today, whole categories of middle-class citizens—writers, actors, musicians and students who are "needy" by choice— sustain themselves off and on for years with unemployment payments. Some significant percentage of this federal job insurance policy is now functioning as a permanent subsidy for those who prefer not to work steadily, many of them clearly describable as middle class.

The largest outlay in the "welfare" budget went to Social Security—$81.3 billion in 1976. Originally conceived as a modest assistance plan to supplement individual savings, an earned right, it is now conceived as a state-financed lifelong pension starting at age 65. The payments go to all who have contributed to Social Security taxes during their working lives. *Most* of the money, consequently, goes to the middle class, which often has other pension systems as well, and to richer people who do not need it. The result is that our Social Security system is breaking down under the strain. It is widely believed that our government pays Social Security out of trust funds which are kept intact and collect interest for precisely that purpose. The public has been deluded. The unfunded liabilities of Social Security add up to more than $4 trillion.

Social Security is often described as the keystone of our welfare system. It is actually a commitment in perpetuity to assist predominantly middle-class citizens, most of whom could very well assist themselves if taxes and inflation—including Social Security levies—were not destroying their capacity to reap the rewards of savings at commercial interest rates.

And even the immense sums I have already listed do not

account for the full $198 billion federal welfare budget. A substantial percentage of it is still unaccounted for—disbursed in hundreds of other health, education and welfare programs. What are they? Most people have no idea. Just as the regulations that govern business attain a high degree of invisibility because of their number, so do these social programs. Only specialists in the welfare field claim to know what they are and what they do, and even these people disagree.

To look at the organizational charts of the great welfare bureaucracies is to know why certainty is impossible. A chart listing federal educational programs is literally indecipherable. Lines—broken and unbroken—of various hues link up little boxes representing various programs. A magnifying glass is necessary to sort out the programs, subprograms and subsubprograms.

All these educational projects exist *in addition* to a nationwide network of government-subsidized public education, public libraries, state universities and community colleges and an extensive scholarship system. In no sense can these extra programs be construed as essential to the survival of the authentically helpless in our midst. Nor, to judge by the scandalously declining literacy rates and national test scores, are they contributing to a rise in the quality of education.

Numerous other social programs also subsidize the middle class. Health, Education, and Welfare Secretary Caspar W. Weinberger discovered that nearly *half* the families receiving benefits from the food stamp program had incomes "well above the poverty level." Similarly, many milk and nutrition programs are not targeted to the needy; the beneficiaries are mainly middle-class children. Day-care programs too are being widely used across the nation by middle-class as well as welfare mothers. Some of the benefits to the middle classes are indirect. The administrators of the welfare programs themselves siphon off some ten to 25 percent of the budgets of these programs in salaries and expenses; they are paid, like all Civil Service employees, at levels higher than those in the marketplace and ultimately receive costly federal pensions for their pains.

So much for the federal welfare budget. There are other programs, but this largely suffices to make my point: Welfare is *not* keyed to the acutely needy among us. It should be cut to the bone, along with the bureaucracies that are placing millions of middle-class citizens on the dole.

In a 1976 lecture at Hillsdale College, M. Stanton Evans made a disturbing calculation. He observed that there were by official definition 25 million poor people in the United States. And he also noted that between 1965 and 1975 the total expenditure on social welfare programs increased some $209 billion to a staggering total of $286.5 billion. He said:

If we take those 25 million poor people and divide them into the $209 billion increase—*not* the whole thing, just the increase—we discover that if we had simply taken that money and given it to the poor people, we could have given each and every one of them a stipend of some $8000 a year, which means an income for a family of four of approximately $32,000. That is, we could have made every poor person in America a relatively rich person. But we didn't. Those poor people are still out there.

What happened to the money? The answer is that some of it did get into hands of the people who are supposed to get it. But a lot of it didn't. The majority of it went to ... social workers and counselors and planners and social engineers and urban renewal experts and the assistant administrators to the administrative assistants who work for the federal government.

While it is not exclusively the bureaucrats who are devouring the bulk of the money, Evans is right when he says that it is not the poor. A growing population of dependents—a growing corruption of the population—is now a vested interest of the egalitarian world. America is not a welfare state even in the old New Deal sense of the term. This country today is purely and simply a redistributionist state, endlessly shaking down Peter to pay Paul. Not orphaned Paul, not crippled Paul, not aged Paul, not black Paul, just *Paul*.

We can now stand back and look at the overall pattern built into our government. Here is what we see: *(1) We see the arbitrary assaults on business and the slow destruction of our productive system, which is the source of all wealth. (2) We see the redistribution of increasing amounts of wealth to a combined clientele of the acutely needy and a growing portion of the middle class. (3) We see the tax burden growing steadily to finance the redistribution process. (4) We see an abyss of governmental debt piled on debt, much of it hidden from the public by budgetary manipulation. (5) We see a commitment to a vast network of lifelong pensions to government employees and others in the middle-class populace.* We see something eerily similar to the fiscal pattern of New York City.

When I said earlier that New York's present was America's future, I meant it seriously. There are differences, of course, between a city and a nation. New York cannot print and inflate money to escape, deceptively, from its debts; the federal government can. The national Ponzi game will go on much longer.

But as our incessantly compounding debt coincides with a nonstop regulatory assault on our productive system and a nonstop redistributionist assault on our productive classes, the national Ponzi game too must ultimately self-destruct. Our government has not been *warring* on poverty; it has been *creating* poverty by attacking every value and every institution on which the generation of wealth depends. And with this, inevitably, it is corroding our liberty. Unless the lethal pattern is changed—which means, unless the philosophy that shapes this pattern is changed—this nation will be destroyed.

VII

The Road to Liberty

All that is necessary for evil to triumph is for good
men to do nothing.
                                                —EDMUND BURKE

There is tragically little awareness in the United States today
that a guiding philosophy lies behind the destruction we are
seeing. There is, however, a substantial awareness in our
political leadership that our fiscal and economic policies have
gone awry and that the multiple promises of cradle-to-grave
security for our citizens can no longer be responsibly expanded,
if indeed they can be fulfilled. What, then, can we do? The *last*
thing to do is to fight conventionally in the political arena, on the
assumption that getting Republicans or conservatives of both
parties into office is a solution. Such men are merely faced today
with a tidal wave of egalitarian projects and proposals for
increasingly authoritarian controls over the economy, and the
best and most principled among them merely find themselves
saying no. The outpouring of Ford vetoes was the most heroic
aspect of his Administration. But consistent negativism is not a
constructive or even intelligible long-range position.

Similarly, one should not come up with programs of one's
own. Not only would they turn out, in the current context, to be
modified egalitarian-authoritarian programs, but also, the very
approach is itself a symptom of the interventionist disease. The
incessant spawning and modification of laws, regulations,
programs and "national purposes" are the expressions of a state
which sees its primary function as a controller of citizens.

What we need today in America is adherence to a set of broad
guiding principles, not a thousand more technocratic adjust-

ments. Let me suggest a few of the most important general principles which I would like to see placed on the public agenda:

—The overriding principle to be revived in American political life is that which sets individual liberty as the highest political value—that value to which all other values are subordinate and that which, at all times, is to be given the highest "priority" in policy discussions. By the same token, there must be a conscious philosophical prejudice against any intervention by the state into our lives, for by definition such intervention abridges liberty.

—The principle of "no taxation without representation" must again become a rallying cry of Americans. Only Congress represents American voters, and the process of transferring regulatory powers—which are a hidden power to tax—to unelected, uncontrollable, and unfireable bureaucrats must stop. The American voters, who pay the bills, must be in a position to know what is being economically inflicted on them and in a position to vote men out of office who assault their interests, as *the voters* define those interests.

—A critical principle which must be communicated forcefully to the American public is the inexorable interdependence of economic wealth and political liberty. Our citizens must learn that what keeps them prosperous is production and technological innovation. Their wealth emerges, not from government offices or politicians' edicts, but only from that portion of the marketplace which is free.

—Bureaucracies themselves should be assumed to be noxious, authoritarian parasites on society, with a tendency to augment their own size and power. People must be taught to start calling for a rollback of the bureaucracy, where nothing will be lost but strangling regulation.

—Productivity and the growth of productivity must be the *first* economic consideration at all times, not the last. That is the source of technological innovation, jobs, and wealth. This means that profits needed for investment must be considered a great social blessing, not a social evil.

—The concept that "wealth is theft" must be repudiated. It now lurks, implicitly, in most of the political statements we hear. Wealth can indeed be stolen but only *after* it has been produced, and the difference between stolen wealth and produced wealth is critical. If a man obtains money by fraud or by force, he is simply a criminal. But if he has earned his income honorably, by the voluntary exchange of goods and services, he is not a criminal or a second-class citizen. A society taught to perceive producers as criminals will end up by destroying its productive processes.

—Similarly, the view that government is virtuous and producers are evil is a piece of folly, and a nation which allows itself to be tacitly guided by these illusions must lose both its liberty and its wealth. Government can be both good and bad. Producers as well can be honest and dishonest. Our political discourse can be rendered rational only when people are taught to make such discriminations.

—The "ethics" of egalitarianism must be repudiated. Achievers must not be penalized or parasites rewarded if we aspire to a healthy, productive and ethical society. Clearly, so long as the government's irrational fiscal policies make this impossible, present commitments to pensions and Social Security must be maintained at all cost, for the bulk of the population has no other recourse. But as soon as is politically feasible—meaning, as soon as *production* becomes the nation's highest economic value—the contributions of able-bodied citizens to their own future pensions should be invested by them in far safer commercial institutions where the sums can earn high interest without being squandered by politicians and bureaucrats. American citizens must be taught to wrest their life savings from the politicians if they are to know the comfort of genuine security.

—The American citizen must be made aware that today a relatively small group of people is proclaiming its purpose to be the will of the People. That elitist approach to government must be repudiated. There is no such thing as the People; it is a collectivist myth. There are only individual citizens with individual wills and individual purposes. It is scarcely astonishing that individuals now feel "alienated" from their government. They are not just alienated from it; they have virtually been expelled from the governmental process.

These are some of the broad conclusions I have reached after four years in office. Essentially they are a set of guiding principles. In fact, these are not particularly original principles. They were the fundamental precepts of American society when the nation was expanding healthily. It is evident today that our nation is being ruled by precisely the opposite principles and that our growing degeneration, both political and economic, is the result of that philosophical reversal.

The single most important thing I can conceive of in the realm of American political life is to make Americans aware that this has happened; that we are careening with frightening speed toward collectivism and away from individual sovereignty, toward coercive centralized planning and away from free individual choices, toward a statis-dictatorial system and away from a nation in which individual liberty is sacred. It is imperative to launch a national "dialogue" on these very issues. They should be publicly discussed and debated in every home.

There is only one way to generate a public awareness of the issues I have listed and to launch a broad challenge of the assumptions and goals presently underlying our political life. What we desperately need in America today is a powerful counterintelligentsia dedicated to the political value of individual liberty, above all, and which is consciously aware of the value of the free market in generating innovative technology, jobs, and wealth.

We have been seeing the birth of just such a movement in recent years, spontaneously generated in three parts of our culture. The oldest, of course, is the educated pro-free enterprise conservative movement. The most brilliant and dedicated intellectuals of the right are classical liberals, adherents of limited government and a minimally regulated free market economy, and are totally aware of the unbreakable link between political and economic liberty. These people have built themselves a fortress in the heart of academe. They have kept the torch of economic liberty burning and are passing it on to younger generations.

The younger generations tend, in fact, to be more militant about the free market than their elders. The most publicly visible are the young libertarians such as Robert Nozick, a philosophy professor at Harvard and winner of a 1975 National Book Award. The libertarians are so intense in their dedication to freedom that their impact on the intellectual world transcends their numbers. Utopian, idealistic and immoderate—to them "extremism in the defense of liberty is no vice"—they are the connecting link between America's free enterprise past and future and refute the canard that economic liberty is a value to rich old men alone.

The second group concerned with liberty has sprung from within the very heart of the liberal world and has become known, however, inaccurately, as "neo-conservative." These people are essentially anticommunist scholars of a New Deal stripe. Some are former leftists; some are affiliated with organized labor. All have gradually become aware that certain components of their own interventionist philosophy are destroying political liberty, academic liberty and jobs. Shocked into an awareness of the destructive trends by the totalitarian instincts of the New Left, they have begun to challenge the most irrational collectivist and egalitarian developments. Among the most prominent members of this group are distinguished intellectuals like Irving Kristol, James Q. Wilson, Nathan Glazer, Daniel Bell, Michael Novak and Sidney Hook.

And the third broad movement in opposition to prevailing trends is to be found in the world of business itself, where the most intelligent and courageous leaders have faced the fact that they must fight for free enterprise before it is too late. The action taken by such men and companies usually consists of public education projects in free market economics and high-powered advertising campaigns in the mass media, where they present the ideas and arguments on behalf of the free market that are conventionally ignored or suppressed by those media.

These three groups are not large, speaking numerically, and their views are by no means uniform. But they have widening spheres of influence in our society, at least in that portion of it which is concerned with ideas. And ideas are weapons—indeed, the only weapons with which other ideas can be fought.

The countermovement I propose should begin with a group of courageous and genuinely principled businessmen who will refrain from asking for one cent of the taxpayers' money, who will honorably accept the risks and penalties of freedom along with its great rewards. Only such a group can earn the respect of the American people and begin to exert a moral influence. Once organized, such a group can start the needed crusade to divert the immense corporate funds presently earmarked for education, "public relations," and "institutional advertising" into the organizations needed to sustain and expand the counterintelligentsia.

What this means is nothing less than a massive and unprecedented mobilization of the moral, intellectual and financial resources which reside in those who still have faith in the human individual, who believe in his right to maximum responsible liberty and who are concerned that our traditional free enterprise system, which offers the greatest scope for the exercise of our freedom, is in dire peril. What, then, will this crusade or this mobilization involve?

1. Foundations imbued with the philosophy of freedom (rather than encharged with experimental dabbling in socialist utopian ideas) must take pains to funnel desperately needed funds to scholars, social scientists, writers and journalists who understand the relationship between political and economic liberty and whose work will supplement and inspire the understanding and the work of others still to come.

2. Business must cease the mindless subsidizing of colleges and universities whose departments of economics, government, politics and history are hostile to capitalism and whose faculties will not hire scholars whose views are otherwise.

This is no interference with the First Amendment rights of the intellectuals presently working in our universities. They remain free as the wind to express the views they choose. It merely ensures that the citadels of anticapitalist thought will be deprived of the funds generated by a system *they* consider to be corrupt and unjust.

3. Finally, business money must flow away from the media which serve as megaphones for anticapitalist opinion and to media which are either pro-freedom or at least professionally capable of a fair and accurate treatment of pro-capitalist ideas, values and arguments. The First Amendment guarantees freedom of speech and of the press from governmental intervention. It does not require that any citizen finance those that seek to destroy him.

These are the three fronts on which to act aggressively if we are to create a sophisticated counterforce to the rising despotism. One of my own first actions on leaving the post of Secretary of the Treasury was to accept the job of president of the John N. Olin Foundation, whose purpose is to support those individuals and institutions who are working to strengthen the free enterprise system. I do this in the fervent hope that my children will have the same freedom, the same opportunities to succeed or fail that I did.

It is often said by people who receive warnings about declining freedom in America that such a charge is preposterous, that there is no freer society on earth. That is true in one sense, but it is immensely deceptive. There has never been such freedom before in America to speak freely, indeed, to wag one's tongue in the hearing of an entire nation; to publish anything and everything, including the most scurrilous gossip; to take drugs and to prate to children about their alleged pleasures; to propagandize for bizarre sexual practices; to watch bloody and obscene entertainment. Conversely, there has never been so little freedom before in America to plan, to save, to invest, to build, to produce, to invent, to hire, to fire, to resist coercive unionization, to exchange goods and services, to risk, to profit, to grow.

The strange fact is that Americans are constitutionally free today to do almost everything that our cultural tradition has previously held to be immoral and obscene, while the police powers of the state are being invoked against almost every aspect of the productive process.

Consider this warning by Professor Robert Nisbet, professor of humanities at Columbia University, included in his essay "The New Despotism":

> A century ago, the liberties that now exist routinely on stage and screen, on printed page and canvas would have been unthinkable in America—and elsewhere in the West, for that matter, save in the most clandestine and limited of settings. But so would the limitations upon economic, professional, education and local liberties, to which we have by now become accustomed, have seemed equally unthinkable a half century ago. We enjoy the feeling of great freedom, of protection of our civil liberties.... But all the while, we find ourselves living in circumstances of a spread of military, police and bureaucratic power that cannot help but have, that manifestly does have, profoundly erosive effect upon those economic, local and associative liberties that are by far the most vital to any free society.

Like others whom I have quoted in this book, Mr. Nisbet stands as a living illustration of what I mean by a counterintellectual. It is only the scholar with a profound understanding of the nature of liberty and the institutions on which it rests who can stand ultimate guard over American cultural life.

I do not mean to imply here that it is only on a lofty, scholarly level that the fight can be conducted, although it unquestionably must begin at that level. At any time and on any social level the individual can and should take action. I have done so in my realm, and you too can work for your liberty, immediately and with impact.

Parents must take an active role in the education of their

children. Join parent-teacher associations; examine the courses and material that your children are receiving. Do not hesitate to protest strenuously. Run for local school boards.

Get involved in politics—in campaigns from the town council to the White House. Support only those candidates who will not waver on the issue of liberty. For too long we have willingly accepted the "lesser of two evils." But the most urgent counsel I can give you is this:

Stop asking the government for "free" goods and services, however desirable and necessary they may seem to be. They are not free. They are simply extracted from the hide of your neighbors—and can be extracted only by force. If you would not confront your neighbor and demand his money at the point of a gun to solve every new problem that may appear in your life, you should not allow the government to do it for you. Be prepared to identify any politician who simultaneously demands your "sacrifices" and offers you "free services" for exactly what he is: an egalitarian demagogue. This one insight understood, this one discipline acted upon and taught by millions of Americans to others could do more to further freedom in American life than any other.

There is, of course, a minimum of government intervention needed to protect a society, particularly from all forms of physical aggression, from economic fraud and, more generally, to protect the citizen's liberty and constitutional rights. What that precise minimum is in terms of a percentage of the GNP I am not prepared to say, but I do know this: that a clear cutoff line, beyond which the government may not confiscate our property, must be sought and established if the government is not to invade every nook and cranny of our lives. In the lowest income groups in our nation there are men and women too proud, too independent to accept welfare, even though it is higher than the wages they can earn. Surely such pride can be stimulated on the more affluent levels of our society.

Ultimately, of course, it is in the political arena that we must definitely solve these problems. The difficulties will be great because Congress today, much of the judiciary, and for the moment the executive are dominated by a coercive, redistributionist, and collectivist philosophy. The Democratic party is the primary vehicle of economic authoritarianism. The only party with a philosophical heritage which might permit it to be the Liberty Party in the United States is the Republican Party. But the Republican Party today is inert—reduced to spineless inconsistency by a half century of compromises on principle. Until its politicians are willing to stand up and fight for freedom with moral conviction and passion, it has no future. The only thing that can save the Republican Party, in fact, is a counterintelligentsia. Without such a reservoir of antiauthoritarian scholarship on which to draw, it is destined to remain the Stupid Party and to die.

It is with a certain weariness that I anticipate the charge that I am one of those "unrealistic" conservatives who wishes to "turn back the clock." There is a good deal less to this criticism than meets the eye. History is not a determinist carpet rolling inexorably in the direction of collectivism. There is nothing "realistic" in counseling people to adjust to that situation. Realism, in fact, requires the capacity to face intolerably unpleasant problems, and to take the necessary steps to dominate future trends, not to be crushed passively beneath them.

The time plainly has come to act. And I would advise the socially nervous that if our contemporary "New Despots" prefer to conceive of themselves as "progressive" and denounce those of us who would fight for liberty as "reactionary," let them. Words do not determine reality. Indeed, if language and history are to be taken seriously, coercion is clearly reactionary, and liberty clearly progressive. In a world where 80 percent of all human beings still live under harrowing tyranny, a tyranny always rationalized in terms of the alleged benefits to a collectivist construct called the People, the American who chooses to fight for the sanctity of the individual has nothing for which to apologize.

One of the clearest measures of the disastrous change that has taken place in this country is the fact that today one must intellectually justify a passion for individual liberty and for limited government, as though it were some bizarre new idea. Yet angry as I get when I reflect on this, I know there is a reason for it. Seen in the full context of human history, individual liberty *is* a bizarre new idea. And an even more bizarre new idea is the free market. These twin ideas appeared like a dizzying flare of light in the long night of tyranny that has been the history of the human race. That light has begun to fade because the short span of 200 years has not been long enough for most of our citizens to understand the extraordinary nature of freedom. I say

this with genuine humility. I came to understand this late in life
myself. But having understood it, I cannot let that light die out
without a battle. It is my profound hope that this book will
inspire the same determination in others.

Epilogue

In the two years since I left Washington, more disheartening evidence has piled up to indicate that, after all, the "bizarre idea" of individual liberty may be too much for Americans to grasp. Despite all the talk about "tax revolt" and people being "fed up" with big government, the majority of Americans are not putting their vote where their mouth is. In the 1978 national elections an estimated two thirds of eligible voters did *not* go to the polls. Those who did go decidedly did not—as the old political dictum goes—"throw the rascals out."

Thumbing their noses at the ideologically vague Republicans, the voters backed a huge number of incumbent Democrats—those Christine Jorgensens of American politics who campaign like George Wallace and vote like George McGovern. This time, they donned tax-cutting fustian and breathed heavily through their Howard Jarvis masks as they ran along the campaign trail. In the aftermath, commentators and columnists pontificated endlessly on exactly what "message" the voters sent. But to me the important and disquieting message was the one sent by the millions of Americans who did not vote. Why didn't they go to the polls? Arthur T. Hadley, author of a recently published study, "The Empty Polling Booth," provided devastating answers. People don't vote, Hadley indicates, because (1) they don't think they can plan ahead in life—everything's a matter of luck, and (2) they feel "politically impotent"—their vote doesn't count.

If, as Hadley discovered, there is an increasing reliance on luck by Americans, there is also an increasing predilection to look upon the federal government as the source of that luck. Think of it. *More than 60 million Americans now get some kind of check from the government! They gather beneath the federal faucet. They agree that it pours forth a torrent, and that the*

handle appears to be missing. But rather than summon a
plumber they jockey for position beneath the stream with
buckets, pans and cups. It was Frederic Bastiat, France's
premier champion of property and liberty, who noted:

> The government offers to cure all the ills of mankind.
> It promises to restore commerce, make agriculture
> prosperous, expand industry, encourage arts and letters,
> wipe out poverty, etc., etc. All that is needed is to create
> some new government agencies and to pay a few more
> bureaucrats.

And thus the terrible circle closes. Government continues to
take from us to give to us (or some of us). These transfer
payments—money sucked out of our paychecks and poured
into the pockets of others—now total more than $202 billion a
year and are growing three times faster than the economy in real
terms. Such awesome largess lies at the root of the government
spending that fuels inflation.

Is it any wonder, then, that we are treated like ignoramuses?
Ponder this somewhat random catalogue of events.

President Carter was only weeks in office when he revised the
Ford budget up from $440 billion to $462 billion. A year later, he
unveiled a $500 billion lulu. Half a trillion dollars! More money
for the scandal-ridden CETA (Comprehensive Employment
and Training Act) program; more money for the education
lobby; more money for Social Security (the biggest tax increase
in history).

Predictably, the dollar has become an international sick joke.
The inflation that was at an annual rate of 4.8 percent when
President Carter took office has now reached over ten percent.
In the midst of the inflation the Congress ruminated, grunted
and finally produced an exercise in casuistry called the tax cut
of 1978. But congressional tax cuts—and this one was no
exception—only appear to do what they say. The complex bill
that finally got through Congress included a record $18.7 billion
in reductions. As most of you should certainly have figured out
by now, however, the reductions were more than offset by
inflation and by sharply increased Social Security taxes. Indeed,
80 percent of the taxpayers are actually paying more than they
did last year.

The much touted Carter energy program which I described

earlier in this book was a circus freak. But its trip through plastic surgery on Capitol Hill turned it into something even more preposterous.

The energy package was supposed to induce Americans to use less energy and rely less on foreign oil. But what came out of the legislative hopper is a confusion rather than an inducement. Nowhere is this more apparent than in the "centerpiece" of the plan—the measure that is supposed to de-regulate natural gas, thus boosting its production and making the United States less dependent on foreign energy. The section is a marvel—a fusion of the sublime *and* the ridiculous. Years of study and litigation are expected before many of its provisions can be figured out. Although styled as a de-regulation law, it in fact imposes greater regulation, extending the hand of government even into the *intra*-state market, which had previously been uncontrolled and therefore highly productive.

All this is in keeping with the increasingly apparent role of the Department of Energy (DOE). This monstrous outgrowth of the old Federal Energy Administration now comprises 19,000 bureaucrats feeding off a $12.5 billion budget, while gas lies in the ground unused because industry can't get permission to transport it. As the *Wall Street Journal* noted, "We now have a giant energy bureaucracy that not only rations scarcity but creates scarcity, thus providing an excuse for its own existence."

So here we are. We have become a nation of abdicators—abdicating the education of our children to an army of social reformers; abdicating the incredible productivity of the free market to redistributionist zealots; abdicating our hopes for old age to a computer that spits out government checks worth less and less in real dollars with each passing month. Weary of vigilance, we are abdicating our very right to govern. And thus we leave a terrible vacuum in which government grows.

Unless we reverse ourselves—unless we eliminate that vacuum—we will lose everything. Do we have the guts to put our own government in its place?